THE PROMISES OF ALLAH ﷻ

SULEIMAN HANI

ISBN: 978-1-969358-00-5
Waymark Publications

contents

preface ... 7
introduction ... 9
1 the roman rebound ... 11
2 the promise of succession ... 17
3 the promise of sacred return ... 19
4 twin promises about the Qur'an ... 25
Divine promises in everyday life ... 31
5 the promise of guidance ... 33
6 the promise of increased blessings ... 42
7 the promise of divine sufficiency ... 47
8 the promise of divine relief ... 51
9 the promise of divine discernment ... 56
10 the promise of answered prayers ... 62
11 the promise of divine support ... 70
12 the promise that charity will be replaced ... 77
13 the promise of a good life ... 83
14 the promise of divine forgiveness ... 91
15 the promise of reciprocal forgiveness ... 99
16 the promise of divine remembrance ... 105
17 the promise of temporary trials ... 112
18 the promise of consequence ... 119
19 the promise of return ... 124
20 the promise of mercy at death ... 131
Promises for the afterlife ... 139
21 the promise of the hereafter ... 141
22 the promise of justice ... 147
23 the promise of safety in the afterlife ... 153
24 the promise of paradise ... 153
25 the promise of eternal reunion ... 167
26 the promise of seeing allah ... 175
27 trust in the promise ... 179
glossary ... 183
index of Qur'anic verses ... 185
about the author ... 189

To our resilient brothers and sisters in Palestine and other lands, who've endured unimaginable suffering and oppression while inspiring millions with their faith in the promises of Allah.

May Allah's promises encompass you in this life and the next.

Transliteration Guide

This is a brief guide to some of the symbols and letters used in the Arabic transliteration in this book.

Consonants

th	ث	ṭ	ط
ḥ	ح	ẓ	ظ
kh	خ	ʿ	ع
dh	ذ	gh	غ
ḍ	ض	h	هـ

Vowels

ā	(aa)	آ ـا
ū	(oo)	ـُو
ī	(ee)	ـِي

ﷺ

May the peace and blessings of Allah be upon him

(ra)
radi Allahu anhu/ ʻanha, /ʼanhum –
may Allah be pleased with him, her, or them

preface

In the quiet hours before dawn, when the world sleeps and hearts awaken, millions of believers around the globe raise their hands in supplication, whispering their hopes, fears, and dreams to their Creator. In those sacred moments, a fundamental question echoes through the chambers of every sincere heart: Does Allah truly hear me? Will He respond? Can I trust in His promises?

This book is born from that universal human longing for divine assurance, the deep need to know that our Creator not only sees our struggles but has made specific, unbreakable promises to guide us through them. After teaching this topic to tens of thousands of students worldwide, and hearing how much the topic impacted their hearts, their resilience, their trust in Allah, and their dedication to keep striving, it was an easy decision to then reformat this into a book that would help thousands more experience the same, by Allah's Will.

Throughout the Qur'an, Allah ﷻ has woven a magnificent tapestry of promises that span the entirety of human experience: from the most intimate personal struggles to the grandest movements of history, from the fleeting moments of this world to the eternal realities of the next. These promises are not mere platitudes or abstract theological concepts, they are living, breathing assurances that have sustained believers through the darkest nights and the most challenging trials.

In these pages, you will discover how Prophet Ibrahim's unshakeable trust in divine promises transformed his moment of greatest trial into humanity's most enduring lesson in faith. You will witness how the early Muslim community found strength in seemingly impossible predictions that later unfolded as historical realities. You will explore how contemporary believers across the globe continue to experience the fulfillment of these same divine guarantees in their daily lives.

Each promise we examine serves as both a mirror and a map, reflecting the eternal nature of human challenges while pointing toward divine solutions that transcend time and circumstance. Whether you are facing personal hardship, seeking guidance in uncertain times, or simply yearning to deepen your relationship with Allah, these promises offer both comfort and direction.

This journey through Allah's promises is ultimately an invitation to transform how we understand our relationship with our Creator. It calls us to move beyond merely believing in His existence to trusting in His active involvement in our lives. It challenges us to see every trial as a pathway to growth, every blessing as a divine gift, and every moment as an opportunity to align ourselves with eternal truths.

As you turn these pages, remember that you are not merely reading about promises—you are discovering your inheritance as a believer. These are not historical artifacts but living realities meant to illuminate your path, strengthen your resolve, and fill your heart with unshakeable hope.

May this exploration of divine promises become a source of light in your moments of darkness, strength in your times of weakness, and joy in your journey toward the ultimate promise of all—meeting your Lord with a heart at peace.

And Allah never fails in His promise.

Suleiman Hani

Introduction

In our journey of faith, we often find ourselves confronting profound questions that touch the depths of our relationship with Allah: How deeply do we trust in His promises? When we raise our hands in du'aa, do we hold complete conviction in our hearts that our prayers will be answered?

As we contemplate our future, do anxious thoughts creep in about what lies ahead? When we reflect on our sins, do we truly believe in Allah's promise of forgiveness? Do we trust with certainty that after hardship comes ease, and that divine support for the ummah is near?

These questions strike at the heart of our faith journey, leading us to wonder: Why do some believers possess such unwavering trust in Allah's promises while others struggle to maintain such certainty? What experiences have they witnessed in their lives that have eliminated all doubt from their hearts? What profound moments of du'aa or life experiences have manifested in ways that forever strengthened their conviction?

The Qur'an offers us an extraordinary treasury of divine promises. As we journey through its pages from beginning to end, we encounter these promises in various forms—some direct (al-wa'd and wa'eed), others as divine proclamations (wa'd Allah, wa'adAllahu). These promises serve not just as spiritual comfort but as living proof of divine truth, especially when we examine how they manifested in the lives of the companions of Prophet Muhammad ﷺ.

1

The Roman Rebound

A World in Turmoil (602-615 CE)

The early seventh century witnessed what appeared to be the inevitable collapse of the Byzantine Roman Empire. Between 602 and 615 CE, the Persian Empire launched a series of devastating conquests that seemed unstoppable. The year 614 CE marked a particularly dark moment as Persian forces captured Damascus and Homs, eventually seizing Jerusalem itself. The conquest was not merely territorial—the Persians destroyed Christian relics and churches, striking at the very heart of Byzantine cultural and religious identity.

Walter Kaegi, a renowned historian of Byzantine history, captured the gravity of the situation: "The virtual collapse of the Byzantine armies between late 610 and 615, the Persian invasion and occupation of Syria, Palestine, and Egypt, and many raids/attacks all revealed the extremely perilous condition of the empire, which endured, although frail."[1]

By 615 CE, the situation had become truly desperate as Persian forces invaded Asia Minor (modern-day Turkey). The Byzantine Emperor Heraclius, facing what seemed to be the imminent destruction of his empire, made what historians called "extraordinary political concessions."[2] According to the historian Sebeos, Heraclius, with the backing of the Roman Senate, offered to convert the Byzantine Empire into a Persian client-state, merely to preserve its right to existence. He even offered Khosrow II the right to install a candidate of his choice on the imperial throne.[3]

The Persian Advance (616-621 CE)

Rather than accept these desperate terms, Khosrow II rejected the offer and intensified his campaign.[4] Between 616 and 621 CE, Persian forces launched new offensives against the Roman capital (615), the Levant (616), and the strategically crucial region of Egypt (619-621 CE). By 622 CE—a year that would prove significant for multiple reasons—historians noted that the "Persians were poised for world dominion."[5]

The Divine Revelation: A Prophecy Against All Odds

It was in this context of seemingly inevitable Byzantine defeat that Allah revealed the opening verses of Surat al-Rūm (The Romans). These verses would become known as the "Roman prophecy," containing divine foreknowledge that would serve as a profound sign for both believers and skeptics:

غُلِبَتِ ٱلرُّومُ

"The Byzantine Romans have been defeated," (30:2)

فِيٓ أَدۡنَى ٱلۡأَرۡضِ وَهُم مِّنۢ بَعۡدِ غَلَبِهِمۡ سَيَغۡلِبُونَ

"in a nearby land. Yet following their defeat, they will triumph" (30:3)

فِي بِضۡعِ سِنِينَۗ لِلَّهِ ٱلۡأَمۡرُ مِن قَبۡلُ وَمِنۢ بَعۡدُۚ وَيَوۡمَئِذٖ يَفۡرَحُ ٱلۡمُؤۡمِنُونَ

"within three to nine years. The ˹whole˺ matter rests with Allah before and after ˹victory˺. And on that day the believers will rejoice" (30:4)

بِنَصۡرِ ٱللَّهِۚ يَنصُرُ مَن يَشَآءُۖ وَهُوَ ٱلۡعَزِيزُ ٱلرَّحِيمُ

"at the victory willed by Allah. He gives victory to whoever He wills. For He is the Almighty, Most Merciful." (30:5)

The Challenge and Response

The prophecy's boldness cannot be overstated. At a time when the Byzantine Empire appeared to be in its death throes, these verses predicted not just survival, but victory—and within a specific timeframe of three to nine (*bid'*) years.

Ibn 'Abbas reported the context of these verses, explaining that the pagans of Makkah initially celebrated the Persian victory, seeing themselves aligned with the Persians as fellow polytheists, while the Muslims hoped for Byzantine success as People of the Book. When Abu Bakr (RA) mentioned this situation to the Prophet ﷺ, he received the emphatic response: "They (the Romans) will certainly prevail."[6]

This led to a remarkable historical moment—a wager between Abu Bakr and the Quraysh.[7] The pagan Arabs, confident in their assessment of the political reality, challenged: "Your companion claims that the Romans will defeat the Persians in bid' years, so why not have a bet on that between us and you?" This was before betting was prohibited, and Abu Bakr accepted the challenge when they proposed a duration of five years.

The Prophet ﷺ's guidance to Abu Bakr about the wager reveals the divine wisdom in the prophecy's specificity: "Why were you not more cautious, Abu Bakr? For indeed *al-bid'* refers to what is from three to nine." He then instructed Abu Bakr to increase both the timeframe (to ten years) in his wager with Ubayy b. Khalaf, a prominent pagan of Makkah. Ubayy was glad to increase the wager to 100 camels as well, demonstrating his confidence.[8]

The Miraculous Fulfillment (622-627 CE)

What transpired in the following years would be recorded by historians as "one of the most astonishing reversals of fortune in the histories of war."[9] Between 622 and 627 CE, exactly within the prophesied timeframe, the Byzantine Empire achieved what had seemed impossible:

- The Roman Byzantine forces recaptured numerous major cities across Palestine, Syria, and Egypt
- In 624 CE, Heraclius's armies destroyed Persian fire temples and one of their main shrines
- By 626 CE, the tables had turned so dramatically that the Byzantines were able to withstand the Siege of Constantinople

The consequences were profound. While the Byzantine Empire emerged transformed beyond recognition, the outcome proved even "more dire for the Sasanians," ultimately leading to the end of the Persian empire.[10] The prophecy's fulfillment fell precisely within the timeline revealed in the Qur'an, from its revelation in the late Makkan period (619-622 CE) to the decisive Byzantine victories of 624-627 CE.

The Impact on Faith and History

When news of the Byzantine victory reached Arabia, it was reported that "many people embraced Islam."[11] The believers rejoiced for numerous reasons:

1. It represented a victory of the People of the Book over polytheists
2. It served as undeniable proof of the Prophet's ﷺ promise and his prophethood
3. It validated the Qur'an as the true Speech of Allah
4. It signaled the decline of Persian power and the rise of Arab influence
5. It coincided with the Muslim victory at the Battle of Badr
6. It strengthened the Muslims' conviction in their faith
7. It served as a prelude to the broader triumph of monotheism over polytheism

The Promise Fulfilled

The chapter concludes with Allah's powerful reminder:

وَعْدَ ٱللَّهِ لَا يُخْلِفُ ٱللَّهُ وَعْدَهُۥ وَلَٰكِنَّ أَكْثَرَ ٱلنَّاسِ لَا يَعْلَمُونَ

"⌜This is⌝ the promise of Allah. ⌜And⌝ Allah never fails in His promise. But most people do not know." (30:6)

Contemporary Relevance: The Promise of Paradise

This historical prophecy strengthens our faith in Allah's greatest promise—that of Jannah (Paradise). When we struggle with our daily obligations and responsibilities as Muslims, we should remember that Paradise is worth every sacrifice:

- Paradise is worth rising for fajr prayer
- Paradise is worth maintaining modesty in an increasingly immodest world
- Paradise is worth the challenges of being a practicing Muslim
- Paradise is worth avoiding what Allah has prohibited
- Paradise would be worth a thousand years of worship on earth

When the people of Paradise finally enter their eternal home and witness its unimaginable beauty, they will say:

ٱلْحَمْدُ لِلَّهِ ٱلَّذِى صَدَقَنَا وَعْدَهُۥ

"Praise be to Allah who has fulfilled His promise to us..." (39:74)

Through studying prophecies like that of the Byzantine victory, we strengthen our conviction that we too, God-willing, will one day utter these words of joy and gratitude. Just as Allah fulfilled His promise about what seemed like an impossible victory on earth, He will fulfill His promise of Paradise to those who remain steadfast on His path.

This prophecy teaches us that victory and triumph are not measured merely by material or worldly standards—they must align with Divine Decree. As the verse reminds us, "The matter rests with Allah before and after." When Allah makes a promise, it will come to pass, even if it seems impossible by worldly standards. Our role is to maintain faith, stay steadfast, and trust in the ultimate fulfillment of divine promises, both in this world and the next.

From Test to Triumph: The Response of the Believers

The way we respond to Allah's promises in times of hardship reveals the true nature of our faith. This principle becomes beautifully clear when we examine how different groups responded to challenges during the Prophet's ﷺ time.

The Qur'an captures this contrast in Surat Al-Ahzab, where we see two distinct reactions to adversity:

وَلَمَّا رَءَا ٱلْمُؤْمِنُونَ ٱلْأَحْزَابَ قَالُوا۟ هَٰذَا مَا وَعَدَنَا ٱللَّهُ وَرَسُولُهُۥ وَصَدَقَ ٱللَّهُ وَرَسُولُهُۥ ۚ
وَمَا زَادَهُمْ إِلَّآ إِيمَٰنًا وَتَسْلِيمًا

"When the believers saw the enemy alliance, they said, 'This is what Allah and His Messenger had promised us. The promise of Allah and His Messenger has come true.' And this only increased them in faith and submission." (33:22)

This response demonstrates the profound understanding that trials themselves are part of Allah's promise. The believers recognized that facing challenges wasn't a contradiction of divine support, but rather a fulfillment of what they had been told to expect. Their faith deepened through the very experience that might have shaken those with weaker conviction.

In stark contrast, we see another response:

وَإِذْ يَقُولُ ٱلْمُنَٰفِقُونَ وَٱلَّذِينَ فِى قُلُوبِهِم مَّرَضٌ مَّا وَعَدَنَا ٱللَّهُ وَرَسُولُهُۥٓ إِلَّا غُرُورًا

"And ⌜remember⌝ when the hypocrites and those with sickness in their hearts said, 'Allah and His Messenger have promised us nothing but delusion!'" (33:12)

This verse unveils a profound psychological and spiritual truth: hardship serves as a crucible that either purifies and strengthens faith or exposes its weakness. The same circumstances that increased the believers in faith and submission led others to doubt and despair.

2

The Promise of Succession

Perhaps one of the most comprehensive and far-reaching promises in the Qur'an is found in Surat An-Nur:

وَعَدَ ٱللَّهُ ٱلَّذِينَ ءَامَنُوا۟ مِنكُمْ وَعَمِلُوا۟ ٱلصَّٰلِحَٰتِ لَيَسْتَخْلِفَنَّهُمْ فِى ٱلْأَرْضِ كَمَا ٱسْتَخْلَفَ ٱلَّذِينَ مِن
قَبْلِهِمْ وَلَيُمَكِّنَنَّ لَهُمْ دِينَهُمُ ٱلَّذِى ٱرْتَضَىٰ لَهُمْ وَلَيُبَدِّلَنَّهُم مِّنۢ بَعْدِ خَوْفِهِمْ أَمْنًا ۚ يَعْبُدُونَنِى لَا يُشْرِكُونَ بِى
شَيْـًٔا ۚ وَمَن كَفَرَ بَعْدَ ذَٰلِكَ فَأُو۟لَٰٓئِكَ هُمُ ٱلْفَٰسِقُونَ

"Allah has promised those of you who believe and do good that He will certainly make them successors in the land, as He did with those before them; and will surely establish for them their faith which He has chosen for them; and will indeed change their fear into security—˹provided that˺ they worship Me, associating nothing with Me. But whoever disbelieves after this ˹promise˺, it is they who will be the rebellious." (24:55)

This verse contains what scholars identify as three interconnected promises:

1. Succession in the land (istikhlāf): The promise of authority and responsibility as inheritors of the earth, following in the footsteps of previous believing nations.
2. Establishment of faith (tamkīn): The guarantee that the religion of Islam would be firmly established, allowing believers to practice their faith openly and completely.
3. Transformation from fear to security (tabdīl): The assurance that the state of fear and uncertainty would be replaced with one of peace and security.

What makes this promise particularly instructive is its gradual fulfillment. The companions witnessed these promises materialize over time, teaching us crucial lessons about divine promises:

First, Allah's promises operate on His timeline, not ours. The early Muslims had to maintain their faith through years of persecution before seeing the first signs of these promises being fulfilled.

Second, these promises come with conditions. Note the crucial qualifier: "provided that they worship Me, associating nothing with Me." This teaches us that divine promises often require active participation through faith and good deeds.

Third, the fulfillment of such promises often arrives in stages. The companions saw different aspects of this promise fulfilled at different times, from the initial establishment in Madinah to the later expansions of the Islamic state.

Lessons for Contemporary Believers

These historical promises hold profound relevance for modern Muslims. They teach us that:

1. Divine promises require both faith and patience. The early Muslims didn't just wait passively for victory—they prepared, strived, and maintained their faith through severe trials.
2. Hardship often precedes fulfillment. Just as the companions faced intense persecution before seeing these promises realized, we should understand that difficulty can be a prelude to divine support.
3. Recognition of fulfilled promises strengthens faith. The believers' response in Surat Al-Ahzab shows how identifying Allah's promises being fulfilled in our lives can deepen our conviction.

Through studying these promises and their fulfillment, we strengthen our conviction that we too, Insha'Allah, will one day utter these words of joy and gratitude. Just as Allah fulfilled His promise about what seemed like an impossible victory on earth, He will fulfill His promise of Paradise to those who remain steadfast on His path.

This prophecy teaches us that victory and triumph are not measured merely by material or worldly standards—they must align with Divine Decree. As the verse reminds us, "The matter rests with Allah before and after." When Allah makes a promise, it will come to pass, even if it seems impossible by worldly standards. Our role is to maintain faith, stay steadfast, and trust in the ultimate fulfillment of divine promises, both in this world and the next.

3

The Promise of Sacred Return

In the sixth year after the Hijrah, the Prophet Muhammad ﷺ saw a vision that would test the faith of an entire community. He saw himself and his companions entering the Sacred Mosque in Makkah, performing the pilgrimage rituals in complete safety—some with shaved heads, others with shortened hair, all without fear. This vision came at a time when the Muslims had been forcibly exiled from their beloved city for six long years, when entering Makkah meant risking death at the hands of the Quraysh.

When the Prophet ﷺ shared this vision with his companions, their hearts soared with hope. Finally, they would return home. Finally, they would circumambulate the Kaʿbah once more. With unwavering trust in their Prophet's vision, 1,400 Muslims set out from Madinah in the state of ihram, wearing nothing but simple white garments, carrying no weapons except the traveler's sword, driving sacrificial animals before them. They were pilgrims, not warriors.

But what happened next would shake many to their core.

The Divine Promise

At the wells of Ḥudaybiyyah, just outside the sacred boundary of Makkah, the Quraysh blocked their path. The Muslims who had left everything for their faith, who had dreamed of touching the Black Stone once more, were told they could go no further. Negotiations began. Days passed. Then came the treaty—a document that seemed to betray every hope they had carried across the desert.

The terms were crushing: No pilgrimage this year. Return to Madinah empty-handed. Send back any Makkan who comes to join the Muslims, but don't expect the same courtesy in return. Even the opening words of the treaty hurt—instead of "In the name of Allah, the Most Gracious, the Most Merciful," they were forced to write simply "In Your name, O Allah." Instead of "Muhammad, the Messenger of Allah," merely "Muhammad, son of Abdullah."

‘Umar ibn al-Khattab, that giant of faith, could not contain himself. He approached the Prophet ﷺ with questions that revealed the depth of communal anguish: “Are we not upon the truth and our enemy upon falsehood? Why then should we accept humiliation in our religion?” The Prophet ﷺ responded with calm certainty: “I am the servant of Allah and His Messenger. I will never disobey His command, and He will never forsake me.”

It was in this moment of apparent defeat, as the Muslims were returning to Madinah without fulfilling their pilgrimage, that Allah revealed the stunning verse and surah that reframed everything:

لَّقَدْ صَدَقَ ٱللَّهُ رَسُولَهُ ٱلرُّءْيَا بِٱلْحَقِّ ۖ لَتَدْخُلُنَّ ٱلْمَسْجِدَ ٱلْحَرَامَ إِن شَآءَ ٱللَّهُ ءَامِنِينَ مُحَلِّقِينَ رُءُوسَكُمْ
وَمُقَصِّرِينَ لَا تَخَافُونَ ۖ فَعَلِمَ مَا لَمْ تَعْلَمُوا۟ فَجَعَلَ مِن دُونِ ذَٰلِكَ فَتْحًا قَرِيبًا

“Indeed, Allah will fulfil His Messenger’s vision in all truth: Allah willing, you will surely enter the Sacred Mosque, in security—˹some with˺ heads shaved and ˹others with˺ hair shortened—without fear. He knew what you did not know, so He first granted you the triumph at hand.” (48:27)

The Miraculous Unfolding

What happened next defies conventional historical analysis. The treaty that seemed like surrender became the greatest strategic victory in Islamic history. Consider the mathematical impossibility of what occurred:

Within two years of Ḥudaybiyyah, the Muslim community grew from 1,400 potential pilgrims to 10,000—a seven-fold increase. More people embraced Islam in those two years than in the previous fifteen years combined. The treaty’s terms, which had seemed so humiliating, created the conditions for Islam’s exponential expansion. The cessation of hostilities allowed peaceful interaction between Muslims and pagans. When the Quraysh could no longer demonize the Muslims as enemies, people discovered the truth of their message.

Exactly one year later, as promised, the Muslims returned to perform their pilgrimage. The vision was fulfilled to the letter—they entered in security, performed their rituals, some shaving their heads, others cutting their hair short, all without fear. The Quraysh, bound by their own treaty, could only watch from the surrounding hills as their former victims circumambulated the Ka’bah in peace.

But the divine wisdom went deeper still. Within two years, the Quraysh themselves broke the treaty by attacking the Muslim’s allies. This gave the Prophet ﷺ the legitimate cause to march on Makkah with 10,000 companions. The city that had expelled them, tortured them, and waged war against them for two decades surrendered without bloodshed. The Sacred Mosque was not just visited—it was liberated forever.

The Pattern of Divine Promises

This episode illuminates profound truths about how divine promises operate in history:

First, Allah's promises operate on divine timelines, not human expectations. The vision was true, but its fulfillment required a process that human impatience could not foresee. When Allah revealed "He knew what you did not know," He was teaching us that divine wisdom encompasses variables beyond human calculation.

Second, apparent defeats often conceal the seeds of greater victories. Every clause of the Ḥudaybiyyah treaty that seemed disadvantageous to the Muslims became an advantage. The prohibition on Muslims going to Makkah meant the Makkans came to them instead, witnessing Islamic society firsthand. The asymmetric return policy meant that every Muslim who went back to Makkah became a living testimony to Islamic values.

Third, divine promises often require human struggle and patience for their fulfillment. Allah could have transported the Muslims instantly into the Sacred Mosque, could have struck down every opposing Qurayshi with lightning. But where would be the test of faith? Where would be the opportunity for human growth, for the demonstration of trust, for the building of character that comes only through perseverance?

The Timeless Questions

This promise of sacred return forces us to confront essential questions that every generation of believers must answer:

Why didn't victory come immediately? Because immediate victory would have been merely physical conquest. The two-year delay transformed a military expedition into a spiritual revolution. It converted enemies into allies, persecutors into companions. Khalid ibn al-Walid, the "Sword of Allah," who had fought against the Muslims at Uhud, embraced Islam during this period. 'Amr ibn al-'Aas, the future conqueror of Egypt, joined the faith. The delay multiplied the victory exponentially.

Why were battles necessary at all? Because this world operates according to consistent divine laws (sunan). If righteousness automatically meant worldly dominance, faith would become a transaction rather than a transformation. The struggles of the believers serve as tests that purify intentions, build character, and demonstrate the sincerity of conviction.

Why did prophets and messengers endure hardships? Because their mission was not merely to achieve political victory but to exemplify the highest human potential. Their patience in adversity, their forgiveness of enemies, their trust in divine wisdom despite apparent setbacks—these became the eternal examples that guide humanity. A prophet who never struggled could never teach us how to overcome our own struggles.

Why were some martyred instead of achieving worldly victory? Because Allah never promised that this world would be the realm of complete reward. Some victories are measured not in territories conquered but in principles preserved. The martyr who dies upholding truth achieves a victory that echoes through eternity, inspiring countless others to live with courage and conviction.

The Liberation of Understanding

This analysis liberates us from two dangerous misconceptions:

The first is the prosperity gospel fallacy—the belief that faith should immediately translate into worldly success. The Ḥudaybiyyah experience teaches us that divine support often comes disguised as difficulty, that the path to victory may lead through apparent defeat.

The second is the defeatist fallacy—the belief that ongoing hardships indicate divine abandonment. The companions who wept at Ḥudaybiyyah, thinking their vision had failed, discovered they were actually witnessing the prelude to Islam's greatest triumph.

The Historical Miracle

From a purely historical perspective, the fulfillment of this promise defies explanation. How does a small community of exiles, prevented from performing a simple pilgrimage, transform within two years into the dominant force in the Arabian Peninsula? How does a treaty of apparent surrender become the catalyst for exponential growth? How does a prophet maintain absolute confidence in his vision's fulfillment even as circumstances seem to contradict it at every turn?

Secular historians can trace the events but struggle to explain the transformation. The Treaty of Ḥudaybiyyah should have demoralized the Muslim community. Instead, it energized them. It should have contained Islamic expansion. Instead, it facilitated it. It should have proven the Prophet's vision false. Instead, it confirmed his prophethood in ways that military victory never could have achieved.

The verse's phrase "He knew what you did not know" becomes a key to understanding divine intervention in history. What Allah ﷻ knew included:

- That peaceful interaction would convert more hearts than swords could
- That Quraysh's sense of security would lead them to break their treaty
- That the delay would allow for the gathering of a force so overwhelming that Makkah would surrender without bloodshed
- That former enemies would become Islam's greatest champions
- That this pattern of apparent setback leading to greater victory would inspire believers through all future trials

The Living Promise

The promise of sacred return was not merely about one historical moment. It established a pattern that reverberates through Islamic history. When Muslims were expelled from Jerusalem, they returned. When they were driven from Spain, the adhan now sounds from mosques in Granada and Córdoba. When colonialism sought to erase Islamic civilization, it emerged stronger and more widespread than ever.

Every Muslim who has been separated from sacred spaces, every believer who has faced closed doors, every community that has endured exile carries within them this promise. Not that victory will come immediately, not that struggle will cease, but that Allah's promises never fail. The fulfillment may require patience that spans years or even generations, but the divine word remains unbreakable.

The intellectual miracle here is not just in prediction but in precision. The verse specifies security, the ritual details of head-shaving and hair-cutting, the absence of fear—all fulfilled exactly as foretold. But it also includes the crucial phrase "Allah willing" (in sha' Allah), reminding us that all promises subsist within divine will, teaching us to align our expectations with divine wisdom rather than human impatience.

Today, when believers face their own Ḥudaybiyyahs—moments when divine promises seem distant, when apparent defeats test faith, when the path to sacred spaces seems blocked—they can remember: He knows what we do not know. And in that knowledge lies the transformation of defeat into victory, of patience into power, of promise into reality.

4

Twin Promises About the Qur'an

Allah's Promises Regarding His Book

In 1972, workers renovating the Great Mosque of Sana'a in Yemen made an extraordinary discovery. Hidden in the space between the inner and outer roofs lay thousands of parchment fragments, Qur'anic manuscripts dating back to the first century of Islam. As scholars carefully examined these ancient texts, a remarkable fact emerged: despite being written within decades of the Prophet's death, separated by vast distances from other early manuscripts, they matched the Qur'an in our hands today with stunning precision.

The Unprecedented Promise

No religious scripture in human history carries the audacious guarantee that the Qur'an makes about itself. While other communities debate the authenticity of their texts, while scholars reconstruct "original" versions of ancient scriptures, while believers wonder which words truly came from their prophets, Muslims hold in their hands a book that came with an eternal warranty:

إِنَّا نَحْنُ نَزَّلْنَا ٱلذِّكْرَ وَإِنَّا لَهُۥ لَحَـٰفِظُونَ

"It is certainly We Who have revealed the Reminder (The Qur'an), and it is certainly We Who will preserve it." (15:9)

Notice the emphatic language. "Certainly We" appears twice, and the divine "We" appears three times in this short verse. This is not a hopeful wish or a human effort at preservation. This is the Creator of the universe taking personal responsibility for safeguarding His final message to humanity.

The Miracle of Preservation

Consider what this promise has overcome. The Qur'an was revealed in 7th century Arabia to a largely illiterate society. It spread across three continents within a century. It was copied by hand for over a thousand years. It survived the Mongol invasions that destroyed libraries, the Reconquista that burned Islamic texts, colonial attempts to replace it with altered versions. Yet today, a child memorizing Qur'an in Indonesia recites exactly what a child in Morocco recites, matching what a child in Bosnia recites—all identical to recitations from Islam's first century.

The numbers tell an astonishing story. Today, tens of millions of Muslims have memorized the entire Qur'an. Not just scholars or religious professionals—farmers, engineers, children, the blind who have never seen a written page. This creates a living backup system that no disaster could erase. If every Qur'an copy disappeared tomorrow, the Book could be perfectly reconstructed from the memories of millions.

Compare this to the journey of other religious texts. The oldest complete Hebrew Bible dates to the 10th century CE—over a millennium after its composition. The earliest complete New Testament dates to the 4th century—300 years after Jesus. But the Qur'an? We have manuscripts from within 20 years of the Prophet's death, and they read exactly like the Qur'an published yesterday.

The Birmingham Manuscript: A Case Study

In 2015, the University of Birmingham made headlines worldwide. Radiocarbon dating of a Qur'anic manuscript in their collection revealed it was written between 568 and 645 CE—during the Prophet's lifetime. The parchment may have come from an animal that lived when the Prophet ﷺ walked the earth. Yet when scholars compared its text to modern printed Qur'ans, they found perfect correspondence.

This is not faith speaking—this is empirical academic analysis confirming a divine promise that was already fulfilled.

The Challenge That Echoes Through Time

But Allah's promises regarding the Qur'an went beyond preservation. In a move that defies human logic, the Qur'an issued a challenge that has echoed through fourteen centuries:

قُل لَّئِنِ ٱجْتَمَعَتِ ٱلْإِنسُ وَٱلْجِنُّ عَلَىٰٓ أَن يَأْتُوا۟ بِمِثْلِ هَـٰذَا ٱلْقُرْءَانِ لَا يَأْتُونَ بِمِثْلِهِۦ وَلَوْ كَانَ بَعْضُهُمْ
لِبَعْضٍ ظَهِيرًا

"Say, ˹O Prophet,˺ 'If ˹all˺ humans and jinn were to come together to produce the equivalent of this Qur'an, they could not produce its equal, no matter how they supported each other.'" (17:88)

This is not poetry challenging poets, though the Qur'an surpassed the greatest Arab poets. This is not philosophy challenging philosophers, though the Qur'an presents the most coherent worldview. This is a comprehensive challenge—produce anything like this book in its totality: its language, its content, its impact, its preservation, its internal consistency despite being revealed over 23 years, its ability to speak to every generation as if revealed for them.

The Attempts That Proved the Promise

History records numerous attempts to meet this challenge, each failure adding to the evidence of the Qur'an's divine origin:

Musaylimah the Liar attempted during the Prophet's lifetime. The Arabs, who were masters of eloquence, literally laughed at his attempts. His "revelations" were so evidently inferior that they became cautionary examples of failed imitation. One of his attempted verses about elephants was so absurd that even children mocked it.

Al-Nadr ibn al-Harith, an eloquent Qurayshi opponent, tried to counter the Qur'an with Persian tales. Despite his storytelling skills, the Arabs recognized the categorical difference. Stories, no matter how well told, could not match the Qur'an's unique fusion of guidance, law, history, and spiritual transformation.

In the modern era, various attempts have been made—the attempts funded by certain missionary groups, various online "modern Qur'ans." Each attempt only highlights what cannot be replicated. They read like what they are: human attempts to imitate the inimitable.

The Living Miracle in Our Hands

But what makes the Qur'an truly inimitable? Consider these interconnected aspects:

1. Linguistic Perfection: Arabic linguists, even non-Muslim ones, acknowledge the Qur'an established the pinnacle of Arabic expression. Its language is neither prose nor poetry but a unique form that combines the best of both. It uses words with such precision that changing a single letter often disrupts multiple layers of meaning.
2. Historical Accuracy: The Qur'an corrects Biblical narratives in ways that align with later archaeological discoveries. It describes ancient Egyptian rulers as "Pharaoh" in Moses' time but "King" in Joseph's time—a distinction historians only confirmed centuries later. The Egyptians did not use the title "Pharaoh" for their rulers until the New Kingdom period, after Joseph's era.
3. Scientific Insights: Without delving into controversial "scientific miracles," even skeptics acknowledge the Qur'an's descriptions of natural phenomena show no trace of 7th-century scientific errors. While contemporaneous texts

described the earth as flat, sitting on a turtle or held by giants, the Qur'an's descriptions remain consistent with modern understanding.

4. Internal Consistency: Revealed over 23 years, addressing vastly different circumstances, the Qur'an maintains perfect internal consistency. No contradictions, no evolution of core concepts, no trace of the changing circumstances in which it was revealed affecting its fundamental message.
5. Transformative Power: The same words that transformed desert nomads into history's most rapid civilization builders continue to transform lives today. Prisoners become philosophers, addicts become ascetics, the lost find direction—all through engagement with this preserved text.
6. Psychological Insight: The Qur'an describes human psychology with an accuracy that anticipates modern psychological understanding. Its descriptions of cognitive dissonance, self-deception, group psychology, and spiritual development read like they were written by the Creator of the human psyche—because they were.
7. Knowledge of the future. Countless promises of future events came true at the time of the companions, which was a cause for many to embrace Islam, as well as promises about events that manifested after the Messenger ﷺ passed away. Knowledge of the future cannot be man-made and automatically dispels the skepticism of the doubtful about where the Qur'an came from.

The above are highly simplified and condensed examples, from hundreds, about how the Qur'an is inimitable and clearly points to God as the divine source.

The Preservation Promise in Action

The mechanism of the Qur'an's preservation reveals divine wisdom in action. Unlike previous scriptures entrusted to specific groups, the Qur'an's preservation became a communal obligation:

1. Memorization: From the moment verses were revealed, companions competed to memorize them. The Prophet ﷺ would recite new revelations in prayer, instantly spreading them to hundreds. Today's tradition of memorization creates millions of walking libraries.
2. Written Record: Despite limited literacy, every revealed verse was immediately written on available materials—leather, bones, parchment. The Prophet ﷺ had dedicated scribes who wrote as he dictated, creating multiple written copies from the start.
3. Communal Verification: The annual Ramadan review, where Angel Gabriel would review the entire revelation with the Prophet ﷺ, established a pattern of communal verification. No individual could alter the text because too many knew it by heart.
4. Divine Protection: Beyond human efforts, subtle divine protection manifested throughout history. Every attempt to alter or replace the Qur'an failed, often in remarkable ways. Colonial powers printed altered Qur'ans; Muslims detected and rejected them. Orientalists claimed variant readings

disproved preservation; deeper study revealed these variants as divinely authorized modes of recitation, not textual corruption.

The Modern Testimony

In our digital age, the preservation promise takes new forms while maintaining ancient patterns:

1. Digital Verification: Computer analysis confirms that Qur'anic manuscripts worldwide share statistically impossible levels of agreement. Variations amount to differences in script style, not content.
2. Global Accessibility: The same text memorized in Nigerian villages can be instantly verified against apps in Tokyo. Technology that didn't exist when the promise was made now serves its fulfillment.
3. Academic Confirmation: Non-Muslim scholars increasingly acknowledge the Qur'an's unique preservation. Orientalist efforts to find an "evolution" of the Qur'anic text have given way to admission of its remarkable stability.

What This Means for Every Muslim

These are not abstract theological points. These promises transform how every Muslim can approach their faith:

Absolute Confidence: While followers of other religions must wonder if they're reading their prophet's actual words, you hold in your hands exactly what was revealed to Muhammad ﷺ. Every verse you recite in prayer matches what he recited.

Direct Connection: Your relationship with the Qur'an is not mediated through centuries of transmission errors or editorial changes. When Allah ﷻ addresses "O you who believe," He speaks directly to you through preserved words.

Intellectual Foundation: In an age of skepticism, you stand on solid ground. The preservation and inimitability of the Qur'an provide rational, verifiable foundations for faith that satisfy both heart and mind.

Active Participation: By memorizing even portions of the Qur'an, you become part of the divine preservation system. Your memory becomes a repository of divine words, participating in a promise made before you were born.

The Challenge for Our Generation

These promises challenge us to respond appropriately:

If the Qur'an is divinely preserved, why do we treat it as one book among many on our shelves? If it is inimitable divine speech, why do we prefer human words? If Allah has guaranteed its preservation for us, what excuse do we have for not engaging with it?

The preservation is not merely about text—it's about meaning, application, and transformation. A preserved Qur'an that is not read, understood, and implemented represents a tragedy greater than loss. We become like those who Allah describes: "The example of those who were entrusted with the Torah and then did not take it on is like that of a donkey who carries volumes [of books]" (62:5).

The Promise That Keeps Its Promise

Today, open any Qur'an app. Compare it to the Birmingham manuscript from the 7th century. Match it against the Sana'a fragments. Check it against the millions who carry it in their hearts. You will find what no other religious community can claim: letter-for-letter preservation of divine revelation.

This is not ancient history—this is a living miracle you can verify this moment. The promise Allah ﷻ made in Surat Al-Hijr continues to fulfill itself every second, in every recitation, in every heart that embraces these eternal words.

When you hold the Qur'an, you hold proof that Allah's promises never fail. The One who preserved His Book against all odds, across all centuries, through all attempts at corruption, is the same One who promises Paradise to the believers, justice for the oppressed, and mercy for the repentant. If He kept His promise about the Book in this world—a promise we can see, touch, and verify—how can we doubt His promises about the next?

The preserved and inimitable Qur'an in your hands is not just a book. It is evidence that when Allah ﷻ makes a promise, that promise transcends time, overcomes every obstacle, and manifests with a perfection that leaves no room for doubt. It whispers to every seeking heart: "If I have kept this promise so perfectly, trust Me with all the others."

DIVINE PROMISES IN EVERYDAY LIFE

5

The Promise of Guidance

Amman, Jordan

The lecture hall fell silent as Professor Hasan closed his well-worn copy of the Qur'an. The discussion on Islamic ethics had sparked an unexpected question from Zayd, a first-year student sitting near the back of the room.

"I understand that Allah guides those who seek guidance," Zayd had said, his voice betraying a hint of frustration, "but I've been trying to become a better Muslim for years. Sometimes I feel like I'm making progress, but then I slip back into old habits. What am I doing wrong?"

Professor Hasan smiled gently. He heard variations of this question countless times throughout his teaching career. Instead of offering an immediate answer, he asked Zayd and the other students to reflect on a beautiful verse from Surat Al-Ankabut:

وَالَّذِينَ جَاهَدُوا فِينَا لَنَهْدِيَنَّهُمْ سُبُلَنَا ۚ وَإِنَّ اللَّهَ لَمَعَ الْمُحْسِنِينَ

"As for those who struggle in Our cause, We will surely guide them along Our Way. And Allah is certainly with the good-doers." (29:69)

"This verse," Professor Hasan explained, "contains one of Allah's most profound promises—a guarantee of progressive guidance that responds directly to our efforts. Notice the beautiful pattern here: struggle first, then guidance. The Arabic word 'jaahadu' implies consistent effort against difficulty. It's not a single attempt, but a sustained struggle."

He then shared a complementary verse from Surat Muhammad:

وَالَّذِينَ اهْتَدَوْا زَادَهُمْ هُدًى وَآتَاهُمْ تَقْوَاهُمْ

"As for those who are ⌜rightly⌝ guided, He increases them in guidance and blesses them with righteousness." (47:17)

"Think of guidance not as a single moment of illumination," Professor Hasan continued, "but as a spiral staircase. Each step you take upward allows you to see further and breathe clearer air. The higher you climb, the more you want to continue ascending."

After class, Zayd approached the professor with new determination in his eyes. "I think I've been expecting immediate transformation," he admitted. "But these verses suggest something different—a journey of gradual growth where each sincere effort creates momentum for the next."

Professor Hasan nodded with approval. "You've understood the promise perfectly. Now comes the beautiful part—putting it into practice."

The Promise of Progressive Guidance

The promise captured in these verses offers a revolutionary understanding of spiritual growth. Allah doesn't simply promise a one-time gift of guidance; He promises an ever-increasing supply that responds directly to our sincere efforts. This creates what we might call a "virtuous spiral" of growth—each step toward Allah makes the next step both clearer and more compelling.

Consider the experience of Sumaya, a medical resident working exhausting shifts at a busy hospital to help her chronically ill father. For years, her prayers had been hurried and mechanical, squeezed between rounds and emergencies.

"One Ramadan, I decided to make a small change," Sumaya shared. "I committed to praying each salah with full concentration, even if it meant stepping away briefly from non-emergency situations. I wasn't expecting much beyond fulfilling my obligation properly."

What happened next surprised her. "After about two weeks, I noticed my heart actually yearning for prayer time. It had transformed from an obligation I rushed through into a spiritual refuge I looked forward to. Without planning it, I found myself making time for short Qur'an readings after Fajr. Then adding more dhikr throughout my day. Each small change made the next one feel natural, not forced."

Sumaya's experience perfectly illustrates the promise in action; her initial struggle led to guidance, which then increased as she responded positively to it. This pattern reveals a profound truth about Allah's method of nurturing our spiritual growth: He meets our efforts with divine support that makes further growth both possible and desirable.

The Starting Point: Sincere Struggle

The Arabic phrase "jaahadu feena" (جَاهَدُوا فِينَا) in verse 29:69 offers a crucial insight about the nature of the struggle that activates this promise. The struggle must be "feena"—in Allah's cause or for His sake.

This distinguishes meaningful spiritual effort from mere self-improvement projects. When we struggle to wake up for Fajr prayer primarily to please Allah rather than just to improve our discipline, we align ourselves with this divine promise. The intention transforms the action from a personal challenge into a sacred struggle that merits divine guidance.

Ahmad, a software developer, experienced this distinction firsthand. "For years, I tried to quit watching inappropriate content online," he confessed. "I made lists of reasons why it was bad for my productivity and relationships. I installed blocking software and tried accountability partners. Nothing lasted more than a few weeks."

The turning point came when Ahmad reframed his struggle. "During a particularly moving khutbah, the imam spoke about striving against sin as an act of love toward Allah, not just self-improvement. This completely shifted my perspective. I began to see my struggle as something I was doing for my relationship with Allah, not just for myself."

This subtle but profound shift—struggling "feena" (for Allah's sake)—activated the promise for Ahmad. "Suddenly, paths opened that I hadn't considered or experienced before. I found spiritual companions who supported my journey without judgment. I discovered deeper fulfillment in prayer that made the temporary pleasures less appealing. The guidance came in ways I couldn't have engineered myself."

The Upward Spiral of Growth

The second verse (47:17) reveals an even more encouraging dimension of this promise:

وَالَّذِينَ اهْتَدَوْا زَادَهُمْ هُدًى وَآتَاهُمْ تَقْوَاهُمْ

"As for those who are ˹rightly˺ guided, He increases them in guidance and blesses them with righteousness." (47:17)

Notice the magnificent equation here: guidance leads to more guidance; good leads to more good. This creates what one might perceive as the upward spiral of spiritual growth, where each positive step creates momentum for further advancement.

Nour, a young mother of three, described this phenomenon in practical terms: "When I first decided to give up backbiting as part of improving my speech, it felt almost impossible. Social conversations seemed to naturally drift toward discussing others, and I caught myself participating without thinking."

She persisted through the initial difficulty, making istighfār (seeking forgiveness) when she slipped. "After about a month, I noticed something changing. Not only was I becoming more conscious of my speech, but I was developing a deeper awareness of other aspects of my character that needed attention. It's like improving my speech cleared space in my heart to recognize other areas needing growth."

This is precisely the "increased guidance" promised in the verse—one area of improvement illuminates others. Nour continued: "What's fascinating is that each positive change made the next one feel more natural. After addressing my speech, improving my patience with my children felt like a natural next step, not an overwhelming new challenge."

The Prophet ﷺ emphasized these growing "steps" when he said: "Indeed, the religion is ease, and no one makes the religion hard upon himself except that it will overcome him. So be upright, draw near [to what is right], and rejoice; and seek help [in worship] with the early morning, the late afternoon, and something from the latter part of the night."[12]

The divine support mentioned here manifests as making the path increasingly accessible as we progress along it. What initially feels like difficult struggle gradually transforms into natural inclination.

When Guidance Transforms Communities

The promise of divine guidance extends beyond individual spiritual journeys to transform entire communities. Consider the remarkable story of a neighborhood in suburban Birmingham, England.

A small group of Muslim families initially gathered for weekly Qur'an study in their homes. "We were just a handful of families trying to create a spiritually nurturing environment in a secular society," explained Imran, one of the founders. "None of us were scholars or community organizers, just regular people trying to grow closer to Allah."

Their sincere struggle to establish this modest study circle was met with unexpected guidance. "Within a year, our small gathering had attracted over thirty families. We had to move to the local community center to accommodate everyone."

But the guidance didn't stop there. Imran continued: "Someone suggested offering free homework help to neighborhood children as a way of giving back to the broader community. This simple idea transformed into a full-fledged educational support program staffed by volunteers from our study circle."

The initiative created bridges with non-Muslim neighbors who began to see the local Muslim community in a new light. "We weren't trying to create some big social movement," Imran emphasized. "We were just responding to the guidance Allah kept sending our way. Each small step revealed the next one."

Within five years, this humble study group had established:

- A thriving weekend Islamic school
- A food bank serving vulnerable community members
- A counseling service for families in crisis
- Regular outreach sessions that dispelled misconceptions about Islam

"Looking back," Imran reflected, "it's clear that Allah was guiding us along paths we couldn't have imagined ourselves. The verse is absolutely clear, when we struggled sincerely in His cause, He opened ways we never knew existed."

The Guidance That Found Adam

Sometimes the promise of guidance manifests in dramatic ways, as in the story of Adam, a former gang member from Detroit.

Adam (formerly known as Christian) spent his youth immersed in street life. "Violence, drugs, hustling, that was my everyday reality," he recalled. "My father was in prison, my mother struggled with addiction. The streets raised me, and I became exactly what you'd expect."

By his twenty-second birthday, Adam had served two prison sentences and survived three gunshot wounds. "I wasn't expecting to see thirty," he admitted. "That's just how it was in my world."

The turning point came unexpectedly. While recovering in the hospital from his latest injury, Adam shared a room with an elderly Muslim man named Hakeem who was receiving cancer treatment.

"This old man had every reason to be bitter," Adam remembered. "He was in constant pain, far from his homeland, with limited English. Yet he radiated a peace I couldn't comprehend. He never missed a prayer, even when the nurses had to help him perform wudu in bed."

Curiosity led to conversation. Over two weeks of recovery, Uncle Hakeem shared his faith with Adam without pressure or judgment. "He simply lived his Islam in front of me," Adam said. "When I asked questions, he answered. When I challenged him, he responded with wisdom, not defensiveness."

Before his discharge, Adam found himself repeating the shahada (testimony of faith) with unexpected tears streaming down his face. "I can't explain it fully," he said. "I just knew I had found something true."

The journey that followed wasn't easy. Adam struggled to break old associations and habits. "But each time I sincerely struggled—really fought against my old self for Allah's sake—new doors would open. A job opportunity. A mentor appearing at the right moment. Housing in a better neighborhood."

Today, Adam works as a youth counselor, helping young men avoid the paths he once traveled. "When I share verse 29:69 with these kids, it's not theory to me," he explained. "I lived it. When I struggled toward Allah, He guided me along ways I never knew existed. And He keeps guiding me, increasing me in understanding each time I take a step toward Him."

Guidance Through Life's Seasons

The promise of increasing guidance takes different forms through various seasons of life, as illustrated by the journey of Sister Khadija.

In her twenties, Khadija focused intensely on acquiring Islamic knowledge. "I was blessed to study with remarkable teachers who awakened my love for the Qur'an and Sunnah," she shared. "That season was characterized by the joy of discovery—each new concept or hadith felt like finding a precious jewel."

Her thirties brought marriage and motherhood, shifting her spiritual journey. "Suddenly, my struggle was less about acquiring knowledge and more about embodying patience during sleepless nights with babies," she recalled. "I worried I was regressing spiritually because I couldn't maintain my previous level of study."

A wise mentor helped Khadija recognize that Allah's guidance was still increasing, just in different ways. "She helped me see that learning to find Allah's presence while soothing a colicky baby at 3 a.m. was its own form of advanced spiritual training," Khadija smiled. "The guidance hadn't diminished—it had adapted to what my soul needed in that season."

In her forties, Khadija faced the trial of losing her husband to illness. "Grief tested everything I thought I knew about my faith," she admitted. "Yet even in that darkness, I discovered dimensions of Allah's names—Al-Latif (The Subtly Kind), Al-Jabbar (The Restorer)—that I had only understood intellectually before."

Now in her sixties, Khadija counsels younger women with the wisdom of her journey. "Each struggle, when undertaken sincerely for Allah's sake, has led to new paths of guidance," she reflected. "The promise has never failed, though the guidance has taken forms I couldn't have predicted."

Her experience beautifully illustrates that the promise of increased guidance remains constant, while its manifestations evolve through life's changing circumstances.

Practical Steps to Activate the Promise

My dear brothers and sisters, how can we actively position ourselves to receive the increased guidance promised in these verses? Here are some practical approaches drawn from both tradition and contemporary experience:

1. Begin with sincere intention (niyyah)

The Prophet ﷺ emphasized: "Actions are judged by intentions, and each person will be rewarded according to their intention."[13]

Before embarking on any spiritual practice, take a moment to consciously renew your intention—that you are doing this for Allah's sake, not for appearance or habit. This aligns your struggle with the "feena" (in Our cause) condition mentioned in the verse.

2. Embrace consistent small actions

The Prophet ﷺ advised: "The most beloved deeds to Allah are those that are consistent, even if they are small."[14]

Rather than attempting dramatic spiritual transformations, focus on sustainable daily practices. A few minutes of focused Qur'an reading each day will activate the promise more effectively than ambitious but abandoned projects.

3. Practice gratitude for guidance received

Allah ﷻ reminds us:

لَئِن شَكَرْتُمْ لَأَزِيدَنَّكُمْ

"If you are grateful, I will surely increase you [in favor]." (14:7)

When you notice positive spiritual changes, consciously thank Allah for them. This gratitude itself becomes a catalyst for further guidance.

4. Seek knowledge with action

The early Muslims understood that knowledge and action are inseparable companions on the path of guidance. Knowledge calls to action; either it is answered or it departs.

When you learn something new about your faith, implement it quickly, even in a small way. This implementation opens the door to deeper understanding.

5. Make du'aa specifically for guidance

The Prophet ﷺ himself taught us to supplicate:

اللَّهُمَّ اهْدِنِي وَسَدِّدْنِي

"O Allah, guide me and make me steadfast."[15]

If the best of creation sought increased guidance through du'aa, how much more should we? Make this a regular part of your daily supplications.

The Light That Never Fades

My dear brothers and sisters, in a world filled with uncertainty and conflicting paths, Allah's promise of progressive guidance stands as a beacon of hope and clarity. Unlike worldly promises that often disappoint, this divine guarantee has been fulfilled in the lives of countless believers across generations.

As we navigate the complexities of modern life—balancing work, family, social pressures, and spiritual growth—this promise offers both comfort and motivation. Our sincere struggles never go unnoticed. Each step taken toward Allah activates a divine response that illuminates the next portion of our path.

The beauty of this promise lies in its accessibility to everyone, regardless of background, education, or natural abilities. It doesn't require exceptional intelligence or special circumstances—just sincere effort in Allah's cause. Whether you're a student like Zayd, a doctor like Sumaya, a mother like Khadija, or someone with a challenging past like Adam, the promise applies equally to you.

As we conclude our reflection on this magnificent guarantee from our Creator, remember:

وَالَّذِينَ جَاهَدُوا فِينَا لَنَهْدِيَنَّهُمْ سُبُلَنَا وَإِنَّ اللَّهَ لَمَعَ الْمُحْسِنِينَ

"As for those who struggle in Our cause, We will surely guide them along Our Way. And Allah is certainly with the good-doers." (29:69)

This is not merely poetic inspiration—it is divine assurance that our spiritual journey follows the principle of positive momentum. Each sincere step creates energy for the next, each struggle opens new horizons of understanding, and each act of obedience plants seeds for future growth.

Take heart in knowing that your path of guidance will continue to brighten as long as you remain committed to the struggle. As the Qur'an beautifully promises:

اللَّهُ وَلِيُّ الَّذِينَ آمَنُوا يُخْرِجُهُم مِّنَ الظُّلُمَاتِ إِلَى النُّورِ

"Allah is the Guardian of those who believe. He brings them out from darkness into light." (2:257)

May Allah ﷻ make us among those who struggle sincerely in His cause, who receive His ever-increasing guidance, and who walk steadfastly upon His straight path until we meet Him.

Discussion Questions

1. The chapter describes spiritual growth as a "spiral staircase" where each step upward allows you to see further and breathe clearer air. Where are you currently on your spiral staircase of guidance? What was your most recent step upward, and what might be your next step?
2. Consider the stories of different individuals in the chapter (Sumaya the medical resident, Ahmad the software developer, Adam the former gang member, or Khadija through her life seasons). Which story resonates most with your own experience of seeking guidance? What lessons can you apply from their journey?
3. The chapter emphasizes that struggling for Allah's sake activates the promise of guidance. Reflect on a current struggle in your life – are you approaching it primarily as a self-improvement project or as an act of devotion to Allah? How might reframing this struggle as something you're doing for Allah's sake change your experience and outcomes?

"O Allah, guide me among those You have guided, grant me well-being among those You have granted well-being, take me into Your care among those You have taken into Your care, and bless what You have given me."

6

The Promise of Increased Blessings

Jakarta, Indonesia

The morning sun filtered through pomegranate leaves as Manal knelt beside her plot in the community garden. At sixty-two, she had been tending this corner for three years, ever since the textile factory closed. Her weathered hands moved gently through the soil, checking seedlings planted weeks ago.

"Assalamu alaikum, Aunt Manal," called Yasir, a university student who worked the neighboring plot. He noticed her examining wilted tomato plants. "I'm sorry about your crop. This heat wave has been brutal."

Manal looked up with an unexpected smile. "Wa alaikum assalam. Yes, some plants didn't survive, but look—" She gestured toward a flourishing corner. "The mint is thriving, roses are blooming again, and yesterday I harvested enough basil to share with three families."

"But aren't you disappointed about the tomatoes?"

She reached for her worn Qur'an, kept wrapped beside her tools. "Let me share something that transformed how I see everything," she said, turning to a familiar page:

وَإِذْ تَأَذَّنَ رَبُّكُمْ لَئِن شَكَرْتُمْ لَأَزِيدَنَّكُمْ ۖ وَلَئِن كَفَرْتُمْ إِنَّ عَذَابِي لَشَدِيدٌ

"And remember when your Lord proclaimed, 'If you are grateful, I will certainly give you more. But if you are ungrateful, surely My punishment is severe.'" (14:7)

A Divine Equation

This verse from Surat Ibrahim establishes what we might call a divine equation—gratitude leads to increase. The Arabic wording is emphatic, using the strongest form of oath. The letter lām in لَأَزِيدَنَّكُمْ ("I certainly will increase you") conveys absolute certainty. Allah ﷻ doesn't say "I might give you more" but "I will certainly give you more."

What makes this promise remarkable is its open-ended nature. Allah doesn't specify the form this increase will take. It might manifest as deeper contentment, improved health, expanded provision, strengthened relationships, or protection from harm. This unconditional promise invites us to discover how Allah chooses to multiply His blessings when we cultivate genuine gratitude.

The Prophet ﷺ embodied this principle perfectly. Despite facing persecution, loss, and hardship, he was described as the most grateful of people, constantly praising Allah in all circumstances. His gratitude wasn't conditional on comfort but flowed from recognizing that every breath, every moment of existence, was a divine gift.

Three Dimensions of Shukr

True shukr (gratitude) in Islam operates on three interconnected levels that transform it from fleeting emotion to comprehensive practice:

First, recognition with the heart (qalb)—acknowledging deep within that all blessings originate from Allah alone. This internal awareness forms the foundation of genuine gratitude.

Second, verbal acknowledgment (lisān)—expressing thanks through dhikr, du'aa, and praise. Our tongues become instruments of gratitude, constantly remembering Allah's favors.

Third, response through action (jawārih)—using Allah's blessings in ways that please Him. This means employing our health in worship, our wealth in charity, our knowledge in teaching, our time in service.

Consider how this three-dimensional approach transformed Ahmed, a physician who narrowly survived a car accident. "During recovery, I realized that feeling thankful wasn't enough," he explained. "True gratitude meant acknowledging Allah saved my life for a purpose, praising Him through increased prayer, and using my restored health to provide free medical care to refugees every weekend."

This holistic gratitude activated remarkable changes. "My practice became more meaningful, my family relationships deepened, and I found joy in work that previously felt routine. The 'increase' Allah promised came not as more money but as more purpose."

The Gratitude That Emerges from Hardship

Perhaps the most powerful demonstrations of shukr come from those facing severe trials. The situation in Gaza provides extraordinary examples of this spiritual resilience. A teacher in a displacement camp shared: "We lost our home, our school, everything material. But every morning, I gather the children and we count our blessings—we're alive, we're together, we have our faith. Their ability to find joy in small things teaches me that gratitude isn't about having much; it's about recognizing what remains."

A doctor working with minimal supplies in a damaged hospital reflected: "When medicine runs low, we thank Allah for traditional remedies. When electricity cuts, we thank Him for daylight. When we lose patients despite our efforts, we thank Him for those we save. This gratitude isn't denial of suffering—it's defiance against despair." These testimonies echo the response of early Muslims who maintained profound gratitude despite persecution in Makkah. Their shukr wasn't dependent on circumstances but rooted in recognizing that īmān itself was the greatest blessing, one that no oppressor could steal.

Breaking the Comparison Trap

One of gratitude's greatest obstacles is our tendency to focus on what others possess. The Prophet ﷺ wisely counseled: "Look at those below you (in worldly matters) and don't look at those above you, for this makes you more likely to appreciate Allah's blessings upon you."[16]

Khalid, a software engineer, discovered this wisdom's power after years of career dissatisfaction. "I constantly compared myself to colleagues who advanced faster or earned more. Each achievement felt insufficient because someone else had more."

His perspective shifted when he began teaching coding to refugee youth. "I met brilliant people who would excel in tech but lacked basic opportunities I took for granted—citizenship, education access, professional networks. One student had been a senior developer but now delivered food while learning English."

"This wasn't about feeling superior but recognizing overlooked blessings. From that gratitude, I became more generous with mentoring, more focused on meaningful work than status. Ironically, this shift led to better opportunities than my previous striving ever achieved."

The Neuroscience of Shukr

Modern research confirms what the Qur'an established fourteen centuries ago: gratitude transforms our experience at every level. Studies document that consistent gratitude practice leads to stronger immune systems, increased positive emotions, improved sleep quality, and decreased anxiety and depression.

A Muslim neuroscientist explains: "Brain scans show gratitude activates regions associated with moral cognition, reward processing, and social bonding. Allah designed our brains to improve through shukr. This isn't coincidence—it's divine design." This alignment between revelation and research reflects Allah's promise:

سَنُرِيهِمْ آيَاتِنَا فِي الْآفَاقِ وَفِي أَنفُسِهِمْ

"We will show them Our signs in the horizons and within themselves." (41:53)

Practical Activation of the Promise

How do we cultivate gratitude that activates Allah's promise of increase? Consider these proven practices:

1. Morning and Evening Adhkar: Begin each day with the prophetic du'aa: "O Allah, whatever blessing I have this morning is from You alone, without partner. So, for You is all praise and thanks." This frames your entire day with recognition of Allah as the source of all good.
2. Reframe Challenges: When facing difficulties, search for hidden blessings. Instead of lamenting a job loss, recognize the opportunity for growth, time for family, or chance to pursue a better path. This isn't toxic positivity but active engagement with Allah's promise that every situation contains potential good.
3. Sajdat al-Shukr: The Prophet ﷺ would prostrate in gratitude upon receiving good news. This physical expression creates a powerful connection between body and spirit, deepening our experience of thankfulness.
4. Gratitude in Salah: Use your sujud—the position where you're closest to Allah—to express specific thanks. Transform prayer from routine into intimate conversation about particular blessings you've received that day.
5. Express Thanks to People: The Prophet ﷺ said, "Whoever doesn't thank people doesn't thank Allah." Make sincere appreciation a daily habit, recognizing others as channels of divine provision.

Building a Culture of Gratitude

The promise of increase extends beyond individual practice. When families, workplaces, and communities establish gratitude cultures, divine blessings multiply collectively.

A family in Malaysia transformed their home dynamics through simple rituals. "We share one gratitude at dinner—initially our teenagers resisted, but now it's our strongest connection point," the father explained. "We also keep a 'blessing board' where anyone can write what they're thankful for. During hard times, it reminds us of Allah's consistent care."

A small business owner implemented team gratitude practices: "We begin meetings acknowledging specific contributions. Within six months, employee satisfaction rose 30%, sick days decreased, and customer ratings improved significantly. The Prophet ﷺ taught that thanking people is part of thanking Allah—we're living that principle."

The Ultimate Transformation

Consistent gratitude practice leads to two profound outcomes:

First, increased success as believers—not measured in material terms but in fulfilling our purpose of knowing and worshiping Allah. Gratitude keeps us conscious of our dependence on Him, deepening our spiritual connection.

Second, genuine happiness that transcends circumstances. The Prophet ﷺ said: "How wonderful is the believer's affair! If something good happens, he's grateful and that's good for him. If something difficult happens, he's patient and that's good for him."[17] This reveals that happiness doesn't depend on what happens to us but how we respond—with gratitude in ease and patience in hardship, both leading to reward.

Allah ﷻ reminds us:

وَإِن تَعُدُّوا نِعْمَةَ اللَّهِ لَا تُحْصُوهَا

"If you tried to count Allah's favors, you could not enumerate them." (14:34)

Our challenge isn't lack of blessings but lack of awareness. The path forward begins with training our hearts to recognize Allah's gifts, our tongues to praise Him, and our actions to reflect our gratitude.

As we cultivate comprehensive shukr, we activate divine increase—not just in material provision but in contentment, relationships, purpose, and all that truly enriches life. Let gratitude become not an occasional practice but our fundamental orientation, the lens through which we perceive and respond to life itself.

Discussion Questions

1. The teacher in Gaza found gratitude amid devastating loss by focusing on what remained rather than what was taken. How might this approach transform your experience of current challenges? What blessings persist in your most difficult moments that deserve recognition?
2. If you were to express thanks for your greatest blessing through action, what specific service would authentically demonstrate your shukr? What's preventing you from starting?
3. The Prophet ﷺ advised looking at those with less to appreciate our blessings, yet social media constantly shows us those with "more." How can we practically implement this prophetic wisdom in our digital age? What specific changes would help you escape the comparison trap?

"O Allah, help me to remember You, to thank You, and to worship You in the best manner."

7

The Promise of Divine Sufficiency

Toronto, Canada

The sun had barely risen when Lisa received the call she had been dreading. Her husband's company was downsizing, and after fifteen years of loyal service, Muhammad had been let go without severance. As she set down her phone with trembling hands, her mind raced: How would they pay their bills? What about their children's education? The mounting medical expenses?

That evening, Muhammad sat quietly at their kitchen table. Despite the devastating news, Lisa noticed an unexpected calmness in his eyes.

"Aren't you worried?" she finally asked.

He looked up and smiled gently. "Of course I am. But I keep remembering what my father told me during difficult times. He would recite Allah's words:

وَمَن يَتَوَكَّلْ عَلَى ٱللَّهِ فَهُوَ حَسْبُهُۥٓ

'And whoever puts their trust in Allah, then He ⌜alone⌝ is sufficient for them.' (65:3)

"My father lived through occupation in Palestine, displacement, and poverty," Muhammad continued, "yet I never once saw him broken. He taught me that this verse contains one of Allah's most powerful promises—a divine guarantee that transcends all worldly uncertainties."

In our modern world, filled with anxiety, economic instability, and constant change, this profound verse offers more than mere comfort—it provides an unshakable foundation upon which we can build our entire lives. This simple yet profound promise appears in various forms throughout the Qur'an, tawakkul itself mentioned in dozens of different instances, underscoring its centrality to our faith.

But what does it truly mean to have Allah ﷻ as "sufficient"?

The Village that Trusted

There's a story of a small village near Sudan. During a devastating drought that had lasted three years, the once-fertile farmlands had transformed into cracked, barren ground. The village's reserves were depleted, and neighboring communities had little to spare.

The village elder, a man named Sheikh Abu 'Ubaydah, called the villagers to the masjid. Many expected him to organize an exodus to the city, abandoning their ancestral homes. Instead, he reminded them of their forefathers who had faced similar trials.

"Throughout our history," he said, "whenever calamity struck, our ancestors turned not to the east or west, but upward. They embodied the words of many scholars who defined tawakkul as the complete reliance of the heart on Allah in bringing the good, and driving away the evil matters of this life and the Hereafter.

That night, the entire village engaged in heartfelt prayer and dhikr. By dawn, dark clouds had gathered on the horizon. By midday, rain poured over their parched lands. The rainfall continued steadily for days, neither flooding nor insufficient, but perfect for rejuvenating their soil.

A visiting merchant who witnessed these events later asked Sheikh Abu 'Ubaydah if he had been certain the rain would come.

"I was not certain *how* Allah ﷻ would provide," the sheikh replied, "but I was absolutely certain *that* He would provide."

The Fire That Could Not Burn

One of the most remarkable historical examples that illustrates the power of tawakkul is the story of Prophet Ibrahim ﷺ when he faced his village's massive fire.

Ibrahim had challenged the idolatry of his people, demonstrating the powerlessness of their deities by breaking them. Outraged, the authorities decided on a punishment meant to prove the supremacy of their gods. The Qur'an captures this momentous scene:

قَالُوا حَرِّقُوهُ وَانصُرُوا آلِهَتَكُمْ إِن كُنتُمْ فَاعِلِينَ

"They concluded, 'Burn him up to avenge your gods, if you must act.'" (21:68)

Imagine the scene: the flames rose high. Yet in this terrifying moment, Ibrahim ﷺ demonstrated unshakeable tawakkul.

Ibn Abbas (ra) narrates that as Ibrahim was about to be cast into the inferno, he uttered words that would become a timeless expression of trust:

حَسْبُنَا اللَّهُ وَنِعْمَ الْوَكِيلُ

Ibn Abbas reported: "HasbunAllahu wa ni'mal wakeel (Allah is sufficient for us, and He is the Best Disposer of affairs)" was said by Ibrahim when he was thrown into the fire."[18]

Allah's response was miraculous:

قُلْنَا يَا نَارُ كُونِي بَرْدًا وَسَلَامًا عَلَىٰ إِبْرَاهِيمَ

"We ordered, 'O fire! Be cool and safe for Abraham!'" (21:69)

The fire, which obeys only its Creator, immediately transformed from an instrument of destruction to one of comfort. Ibrahim emerged unharmed, providing a timeless testimony to Allah's promise of sufficiency.

Active Trust in Daily Life

When Muhammad and Lisa turned to prayer that difficult evening, something remarkable happened. The anxiety constricting their chests gradually loosened. Not because their circumstances had changed—their financial challenges remained real—but because their perspective had shifted.

This transformation is the natural consequence of genuine tawakkul. When we internalize Allah's promise of sufficiency, our relationship with uncertainty fundamentally changes. Thus, the condensed definition many scholars have given is that tawakkul is the complete reliance of the heart on Allah in bringing good and driving away evil matters of this life and the Hereafter.

Consider this: If the Prophet Muhammad ﷺ asked you to follow him without explaining the destination, would your heart be troubled by the unknown path? Or would his presence as your guide fill you with complete assurance? This thought experiment reveals the depth of our trust in Allah's guidance. How much more should we trust Al-Hakeem (The All-Wise), Al-Khabeer (The All-Aware)?

Building Deeper Trust

The path to developing tawakkul begins with knowing Allah through His attributes and actions. Just as we wouldn't entrust valuables to a stranger, our hearts require familiarity with Allah to fully rely on Him. This knowledge comes through studying the Qur'an, contemplating His names, and recognizing His role in our daily lives.

Consider Maryam (AS) experiencing labor pains alone under a palm tree. In that moment of extreme vulnerability, Allah ﷻ instructed her:

فَكُلِي وَاشْرَبِي وَقَرِّي عَيْنًا

"So eat, drink, and be contented." (19:26)

Even in a challenging moment, Allah directed her attention to immediate blessings and assured her of His sufficiency. This guidance applies to us in trials, that there remain blessings to recognize and reasons for contentment in Allah's care.

The Promise That Never Fails

As we navigate modern life's complexities, Allah's promise of sufficiency remains our most reliable anchor. Whether facing global crises, personal hardships, or opposition to our faith, this divine guarantee offers transformative power.

Remember: Allah doesn't merely promise to help us—He promises to be enough for us. Complete and perfect in every way that matters. When everything else fails, when all doors seem closed, when challenges appear insurmountable, Allah's sufficiency remains constant, unwavering, and perfect.

As we strengthen our tawakkul, we experience profound rewards: greater peace of mind, increased resilience, sustained hope, and deeper spiritual connection with Allah. These aren't abstract concepts but lived realities for those who embrace divine trust.

My dear brothers and sisters, let us live each day in the light of this magnificent promise, secure in the knowledge that the One who holds the universe in perfect balance has guaranteed His sufficiency to those who place their trust in Him.

Discussion Questions

1. How can we distinguish between genuine tawakkul and passive resignation in our own lives? What practical steps demonstrate active trust while maintaining complete reliance on Allah?
2. Ibrahim facing the fire found peace through reciting "HasbunAllahu wa ni'mal wakeel." Why do you think this specific declaration has such transformative power in moments of extreme fear? How might regularly practicing this dhikr in smaller challenges prepare us for life's major trials?
3. How does genuine trust in Allah change our outward demeanor and interactions? Can you share an experience where your internal spiritual state affected an unexpected outcome?

*"Sufficient for me is Allah; there is no deity except Him.
On Him I have relied, and He is the Lord of the Great Throne."*

8

The Promise of Divine Relief

Kuala Lumpur, Malaysia

Yasmin sat at her kitchen table, staring at the final divorce papers. After twelve years of marriage, she was now a single mother of two young children in a city far from her family. The weight of responsibility pressed down on her shoulders like a physical burden. How would she provide for her children? Where would they live now that they couldn't afford their apartment? The questions swirled in her mind like a gathering storm.

That evening, as she tucked her children into bed, her seven-year-old daughter Aisha noticed her mother's reddened eyes.

"Are you sad, Mama?" she asked.

Yasmin managed a small smile. "A little, sweetheart. But do you know what my grandmother always told me? She said that when we're stuck in a dark tunnel and can't see the way forward, Allah always creates an exit we couldn't see before."

"Like a secret door?" Aisha asked, her eyes widening.

"Exactly like that," Yasmin replied, suddenly remembering the verses her own mother had recited to her during difficult times:

وَمَن يَتَّقِ ٱللَّهَ يَجْعَل لَّهُۥ مَخْرَجًا

"And whoever is mindful of Allah, He will make a way out for them," (65:2)

وَيَرْزُقْهُ مِنْ حَيْثُ لَا يَحْتَسِبُ

"and provide for them from sources they could never imagine." (65:3)

As she recited these words, something shifted inside Yasmin's heart. The verses weren't just beautiful in sound, they were a divine promise, guaranteed by the Creator of the universe.

In a world where promises are often broken and guarantees come with fine print, Allah's assurance of relief and provision stands as an unshakable certainty. What makes this particular promise so powerful is its placement in Surat At-Talaq, a chapter dealing with one of life's most painful transitions—divorce. Even in our darkest moments, when relationships fracture and futures seem uncertain, the path of taqwā leads to unexpected openings.

What Does It Mean to Have Taqwa?

Before we explore more examples of this promise in action, let's understand what taqwā truly means. Often translated as "God-consciousness" or "mindfulness of Allah," taqwā goes deeper than mere awareness of the Divine.

Taqwa was described by one teacher as acting in obedience to Allah, upon light from Allah, hoping for reward from Allah, and avoiding disobedience to Allah, fearing punishment from Allah.

In simpler terms, taqwā means:

1. Being aware that Allah sees everything we do
2. Making choices based on what pleases Him, not just what pleases others
3. Avoiding what He has forbidden, even when no one else is watching
4. Remembering His presence in both good times and bad

The Prophet ﷺ beautifully explained taqwā by pointing to his chest three times and saying: "Taqwa is here, taqwā is here, taqwā is here."[19]

This indicates that true taqwā resides in the heart, it's an internal state that manifests in our external actions.

The Unexpected Job Offer

Let me share the story of Kareem, a software engineer who lost his job during a massive tech industry layoff. With a family to support and rent to pay, Kareem found himself sending out job applications daily, with very few responses.

"The rejection emails became so routine that I created a special folder for them," he recalled with a wry smile. "But through it all, I tried to maintain my five daily prayers, even when interviews conflicted with prayer times. I would politely ask for a few minutes to fulfill my religious obligation."

Kareem noticed that some interviewers seemed uncomfortable with his prayer requests, and he worried this might be hurting his chances. Still, he remained committed to prioritizing his relationship with Allah.

"One day, I had a second-round interview with a promising company," Kareem shared. "When Asr prayer time came, I respectfully asked for a brief pause. To my surprise, the interviewer, a non-Muslim woman named Sarah, not only agreed but seemed genuinely impressed by my commitment."

Three days later, Kareem received a call with a job offer. The position offered better pay and more flexibility than his previous role. When he later asked Sarah why they had selected him from among more qualified candidates, her answer stunned him.

"She told me that when I excused myself for prayer, it demonstrated that I was a person of principle who wouldn't compromise on my values," Kareem explained. "She said the company wanted people with that kind of integrity."

The provision came from where he never expected, through the very practice that he feared might hinder his job search. This is the essence of Allah's promise:

وَيَرْزُقْهُ مِنْ حَيْثُ لَا يَحْتَسِبُ

"and provide for them from sources they could never imagine." (65:3)

The Single Mother's Journey

Let's return to Yasmin. After her divorce, she embarked on what she called a "taqwā journey"—making conscious decisions to strengthen her relationship with Allah while navigating single motherhood. She improved her prayer quality, started a gratitude journal, and committed to speaking respectfully about her ex-husband in front of their children.

The financial strain was overwhelming. Her part-time job barely covered necessities. Then, through a chance conversation at her son's school, she learned the Islamic center needed an administrative assistant. Though she applied with little hope, she was hired. Within a year, she was promoted to outreach coordinator.

"The most unexpected blessing came through the Islamic center's network," Yasmin shared. "A widow in the community offered us reduced rent in exchange for light property management duties. Each solution came from a direction I never would have planned."

Taqwa in Gaza: Finding Light in Darkness

Even in the most challenging circumstances, the promise holds true. Dr. Farhan, a physician in Gaza, described how medical supplies arrived through previously unknown humanitarian corridors just when stocks reached critically low levels.

"We maintained our prayers in the hospital despite everything," he recounted. "One morning after Fajr, we received word that desperately needed supplies had somehow made it through. The timing and route defied all expectations."

This reflects a profound truth: the promise of relief through taqwā doesn't guarantee an immediate end to suffering, but ensures that Allah creates openings even in seemingly impossible situations.

Practical Steps to Increase Taqwa

How can we cultivate this taqwā that unlocks divine relief in our own lives? Here are some practical steps drawn from the Qur'an and Sunnah:

1. Remember Allah's presence

The Prophet ﷺ advised us: "Be mindful of Allah wherever you are."[20] This means carrying the awareness of Allah throughout our day, while driving in traffic, scrolling through social media, or having difficult conversations.

2. Guard your tongue

In a time when online arguments and gossip are normalized, controlling what we say becomes a powerful form of taqwā. The Prophet ﷺ taught: "Whoever believes in Allah and the Last Day should speak good or remain silent."[21]

3. Seek Allah's help with patience and prayer

وَاسْتَعِينُوا بِالصَّبْرِ وَالصَّلَاةِ

"And seek help through patience and prayer." (2:45)

When Yasmin from our opening story felt overwhelmed, she strengthened her salah instead of neglecting it. This reconnection with Allah became her anchor during turbulent times.

4. Make halal choices, even when difficult

In a society where cutting corners is often rewarded, choosing the halal path, in business dealings, relationships, and entertainment, distinguishes those with true taqwā. The Prophet ﷺ said: "Leave what makes you doubt for what does not make you doubt."[22]

5. Act with excellence (Iḥsān)

Ihsan is described in the hadith as: "To worship Allah as if you see Him, and if you do not see Him, then He sees you."[23] This consciousness transforms ordinary actions into expressions of taqwā.

The Promise That Sustains Us

As we navigate life's challenges, economic uncertainty, family difficulties, health crises, Allah's promise of relief through taqwā remains our greatest source of hope.

Remember that this promise appears in Surat Al-Talāq, a chapter dealing with one of life's most painful transitions. Even in our darkest moments, the path of taqwā leads to unexpected openings.

وَمَن يَتَّقِ اللَّهَ يَجْعَل لَّهُ مَخْرَجًا وَيَرْزُقْهُ مِنْ حَيْثُ لَا يَحْتَسِبُ

"And whoever is mindful of Allah, He will make a way out for them, and provide for them from sources they could never imagine." (65:2-3)

This is not a conditional promise, it is a divine guarantee. The relief may not come when we want it, but it will come when we need it most. As we increase in taqwā, Allah opens doors where there appeared to be only walls.

Discussion Questions

1. Think about a time when you faced a significant challenge. How did practicing taqwā help you through it?
2. Has Allah ever provided for you from an unexpected source in a manner that's obvious to you? How did this experience affect your faith?
3. The chapter mentions that "sometimes the 'way out' is not an escape from difficult circumstances but a transformation of our response to them." Reflect on a situation where your circumstances didn't change, but your perspective or reaction did. How was this internal shift a form of divine relief?
4. Which of the five practical steps to increase taqwā resonates most with you right now, and why? (Remembering Allah's presence, guarding your tongue, seeking help through patience and prayer, making halal choices, or acting with excellence/ihsan). What specific action can you take this week to strengthen this aspect of taqwā in your life?

"O Allah, make my affairs easy for me, grant me relief from every worry, and a way out from every difficulty."

9

The Promise of Divine Discernment

Sarajevo, Bosnia

Professor Malik had been teaching Islamic studies at the university for over twenty years. His classes were consistently oversubscribed, not for their easiness, as he was known as a demanding instructor, but for the clarity and wisdom he brought to complex subjects. His students often remarked that he had an almost uncanny ability to cut through confusion and identify the core of any issue.

After one particularly illuminating lecture on ethics in ambiguous situations, a graduate student approached him. "Professor Malik," she began, "I've studied with many scholars, but some have a unique way of seeing through complexity. How did they develop this discernment?"

The professor smiled gently. "What you're asking about isn't primarily intellectual," he replied. "The kind of clarity you're describing comes from a divine gift mentioned in the Qur'an, the furqān."

He unlocked his smartphone and opened his Qur'an app to the verse:

يَا أَيُّهَا الَّذِينَ آمَنُوا إِن تَتَّقُوا اللَّهَ يَجْعَل لَّكُمْ فُرْقَانًا
وَيُكَفِّرْ عَنكُمْ سَيِّئَاتِكُمْ وَيَغْفِرْ لَكُمْ ۗ وَاللَّهُ ذُو الْفَضْلِ الْعَظِيمِ

"O you who believe! If you fear Allah, He will grant you a Furqān (criterion to distinguish between right and wrong), remove your evil deeds from you, and forgive you. And Allah is the possessor of great bounty." (8:29)

"This verse contains a profound divine promise," Professor Malik continued. "The Arabic word 'furqān' comes from the root 'fa-ra-qa,' meaning to separate or distinguish between things. Allah promises those who cultivate taqwā, consciousness and fear of Him, a special kind of discernment that allows them to distinguish truth from falsehood, beneficial from harmful, and right from wrong."

The student considered this for a moment. "Is this 'furqān' something different from knowledge or intelligence?"

"Absolutely," the professor nodded. "I've known brilliant professors who lacked this discernment, and simple people with little formal education who possessed it in abundance. Academic knowledge, while valuable, is different from this divinely granted discernment. The furqān is a light that Allah places in the heart, illuminating the path ahead when others find themselves in darkness."

Understanding the Divine Promise of Furqān

The promise contained in verse 8:29 of the Qur'an establishes a direct relationship between taqwā (God-consciousness) and furqān (discernment). This relationship reveals a profound spiritual principle: our moral and spiritual state directly affects our cognitive abilities and perception of reality.

The great companion Ibn Abbas explained furqān as "a way out from difficulties and a light to help navigate through uncertainties." This interpretation emphasizes the practical nature of this divine gift, it provides clarity precisely when confusion is greatest.

Ibn al-Qayyim elaborated, describing firāsah (a similar concept) as "a light that Allah places in the heart of His servant, by which he can distinguish between truth and falsehood, guidance and misguidance, beneficial knowledge and that which does not benefit, and between the path of happiness and the path of misery."[24]

This divine discernment operates across multiple dimensions:

- Intellectual discernment - The ability to distinguish truth from falsehood in matters of belief and thought
- Moral discernment - Clarity about right and wrong in complex ethical situations
- Spiritual discernment - Recognition of what brings one closer to or further from Allah
- Practical discernment - Wisdom in daily decisions and life choices

What makes this promise particularly remarkable is that it establishes taqwā—not intelligence, education, or social position—as the primary prerequisite for this invaluable gift.

Taqwa: The Key that Unlocks Discernment

To understand how to access this promised discernment, we must first emphasize what Allah means by taqwā in this context, as explained previously.

A man once asked Abu Hurayrah (ra) to explain taqwā. Abu Hurayrah responded with a question: "Have you ever walked on a path with thorns?" When 'Umar said yes, Abu Hurayrah asked, "What did you do?" 'Umar replied that he gathered his garment and watched carefully where he stepped. That is taqwā.[25]

This beautiful analogy captures the essence of taqwā—moving through life with careful awareness, protecting oneself from spiritual harm by being vigilant and mindful.

The connection between taqwā and furqān becomes clearer when we consider how taqwā affects our perception and judgment:

- Taqwa purifies the heart - The Prophet ﷺ pointed to his chest and said: "Taqwa is here, taqwā is here."[26] A heart purified through God-consciousness becomes a clearer receptor for divine guidance.
- Taqwa reduces the influence of desires - When personal wants and ego do not cloud judgment, reality becomes easier to perceive accurately.
- Taqwa establishes the correct standard of judgment - When Allah's pleasure becomes the primary criterion for decisions, confusion diminishes.
- Taqwa creates spiritual alertness - The God-conscious person develops a sensitivity to subtle spiritual realities that others might miss.

Furqān in the Lives of the Companions

The transformative power of this promised discernment is vividly illustrated in the lives of the Prophet's companions, who were often people of ordinary backgrounds and limited formal education, yet displayed extraordinary wisdom after embracing taqwā.

Consider Abu Bakr al-Siddiq (ra), whose discernment was so aligned with truth that Umar (ra) said: "If the faith of Abu Bakr were weighed against the faith of all people on earth, his would outweigh theirs."

This furqān manifested dramatically when the Prophet Muhammad ﷺ passed away and confusion spread among the Muslims. Some companions, including the formidable 'Umar (ra), were initially unable to accept this reality. In this moment of community crisis, Abu Bakr (ra) displayed remarkable clarity, addressing the people with the now-famous words: "Whoever worshipped Muhammad, Muhammad has died. But whoever worships Allah, Allah is Ever-Living and shall never die." He then recited the Qur'anic verse:

وَمَا مُحَمَّدٌ إِلَّا رَسُولٌ قَدْ خَلَتْ مِن قَبْلِهِ الرُّسُلُ ۚ أَفَإِن مَّاتَ أَوْ قُتِلَ انقَلَبْتُمْ عَلَىٰ أَعْقَابِكُمْ

"Muhammad is not but a messenger. [Other] messengers have passed on before him. So if he was to die or be killed, would you turn back on your heels [to unbelief]?" (3:144)

Upon hearing this, clarity returned to the companions. Umar (ra) later remarked that it was as if he had never heard this verse before that moment, despite having known it well.

This incident demonstrates how furqān operates in real-world crises—providing clarity precisely when confusion is greatest, and often manifesting as the ability to apply known truths to new situations with wisdom.

Developing the Prerequisites for Furqān

If taqwā is the key that unlocks divine discernment, how do we cultivate this essential quality?

First, meaningful taqwā begins with knowledge of what Allah requires and prohibits. Without proper understanding of divine guidance, one cannot properly fear or be conscious of Allah.

Second, the practice of muḥāsabah, regularly examining one's actions and intentions, helps develop the internal awareness characteristic of taqwā. As is sometimes attributed to 'Umar ibn al-Khattab (ra): "Call yourselves to account before you are called to account."[27] This entails regular accountability, deep reflection, and, for those who benefit from it, practically tracking one's goals and progress in acts of worship that are not yet regular habits.

Third, consistent remembrance of Allah (dhikr) maintains awareness of His presence, which is the essence of taqwā. Regular dhikr, whether through tasbīḥ, Qur'an recitation, or maintaining awareness throughout daily activities, establishes the God-consciousness that leads to discernment.

Finally, surrounding ourselves with people of taqwā helps reinforce God-consciousness, creating an environment conducive to developing discernment.

The Prophet ﷺ emphasized the influence of companionship when he said: "A person follows the religion of his close friend, so let each of you look carefully at whom he befriends."[28] Surrounding ourselves with people of taqwā helps reinforce God-consciousness in our own lives, creating an environment conducive to developing discernment.

Obstacles to Furqān

Understanding what blocks divine discernment is as important as knowing how to cultivate it. Several factors can prevent us from receiving or recognizing this gift:

1. Persistent Sin

The Prophet ﷺ explained the spiritual impact of sin: "When a servant commits a sin, a dark spot appears on his heart. If he abandons the sin, seeks forgiveness, and repents, his heart is polished. But if he returns to the sin, the darkness grows until it covers his heart."[29]

This hadith describes how persistent sin without repentance gradually darkens the heart, diminishing its capacity to receive and recognize divine guidance.

2. Attachment to Worldly Desires

Excessive concern with worldliness distorts judgment. Allah warns:

أَفَرَأَيْتَ مَنِ اتَّخَذَ إِلَٰهَهُ هَوَاهُ وَأَضَلَّهُ اللَّهُ عَلَىٰ عِلْمٍ وَخَتَمَ عَلَىٰ سَمْعِهِ وَقَلْبِهِ وَجَعَلَ عَلَىٰ بَصَرِهِ غِشَاوَةً

"Have you seen the one who takes his own desires as his god? Allah has knowingly led him astray and sealed his hearing and heart and placed over his vision a veil." (45:23)

When personal desire becomes the primary motivation, it compromises the ability to perceive truth objectively.

3. Arrogance and Self-Sufficiency

Allah repeatedly warns against arrogance, which creates a sense of self-sufficiency that blocks divine guidance.

سَأَصْرِفُ عَنْ آيَاتِيَ الَّذِينَ يَتَكَبَّرُونَ فِي الْأَرْضِ بِغَيْرِ الْحَقِّ

"I will turn away from My signs those who are arrogant upon the earth without right." (7:146)

Humility, recognizing one's need for divine guidance, is essential for receiving the gift of furqān.

Furqān in Modern Challenges

In our complex age, divine discernment becomes particularly valuable:

Information Overload. In an era of misinformation and echo chambers, those with furqān develop a "spiritual filter" that helps them navigate competing narratives. Zaynab, a journalist, describes: "Maintaining my prayers and Qur'an reading creates an inner compass. Sometimes I feel inexplicable discomfort with a source that later proves problematic. This doesn't replace journalistic methods but complements them with discernment that transcends pure rationality."

Ethical Technology. Dr. Abdulazeez, working in AI ethics, notes: "Maintaining taqwā—particularly through night prayers when working on difficult problems—provides insights that wouldn't emerge from technical analysis alone. It helps identify subtle harms or benefits that metrics might miss."

Cultural Navigation. Muslims living as minorities face daily questions about integration. Those with strong taqwā display remarkable balance, neither rejecting everything from surrounding culture nor uncritically absorbing it. They show nuance in discerning what to adopt, adapt, or avoid.

The Promise That Illuminates

The divine promise of furqān holds special significance among Allah's guarantees to believers. While other promises address specific blessings, this promise provides the very discernment needed to recognize and value all other divine guidance.

In a world of moral complexity and information overload, the ability to distinguish between right and wrong, truth and falsehood becomes more precious than ever. Allah's promise to grant this discernment to those who fear Him offers clarity that transcends human reasoning alone. This gift is not reserved for the scholarly elite but is available to any believer who cultivates genuine God-consciousness. Throughout Islamic history, ordinary people have displayed extraordinary wisdom because of their taqwā.

As we navigate modern complexities, let us remember this profound promise.

May Allah grant us the taqwā that leads to clear discernment, that we may navigate our world with wisdom and walk confidently on the straight path.

Discussion Questions

1. Reflect on a situation where you faced moral or spiritual confusion. What role did taqwā (God-consciousness) play in helping or hindering your discernment in that moment? How might strengthening your taqwā change your approach to similar situations in the future?
2. The chapter mentions several obstacles to furqān, including persistent sin, attachment to worldly desires, and arrogance. Which of these do you find most challenging in your own life, and what practical steps could you take to address this obstacle?
3. Divine discernment (furqān) is described as different from knowledge or intelligence. Have you observed examples of people with seemingly ordinary education who nonetheless display remarkable wisdom and clarity in their decisions? What qualities did they possess that might relate to the furqān described in this chapter?

"O Allah, show me the truth as truth and grant me the ability to follow it, and show me falsehood as falsehood and grant me the ability to avoid it."

10

The Promise of Answered Prayers

Dublin, Ireland

Sara sat alone in her car, tears streaming down her face. The rejection letter from her dream medical school, the fourth one this month, lay crumpled in her lap. For three years, she had poured everything into this goal: volunteering at hospitals, studying until dawn, repeatedly taking entrance exams to improve her scores. Each application season ended the same way, rejection after rejection.

"I don't understand," she whispered, her voice breaking. "I've prayed for this every day. I've done everything right. Why isn't Allah answering me?"

That evening, Sara called her uncle, a man known for his wisdom and deep faith. After listening to her story, he asked a simple question: "Do you believe Allah hears you when you make du'aa?"

"Of course," Sara replied immediately.

"And do you believe He is capable of getting you into medical school?"

"Yes, absolutely."

"Then what do you think is happening?" her uncle asked gently.

Sara hesitated. "I... I don't know. It feels like my prayers are hitting a ceiling."

Her uncle's voice softened. "When I was about your age, I memorized a verse that changed how I understood du'aa forever. Allah says:

وَقَالَ رَبُّكُمُ ادْعُونِي أَسْتَجِبْ لَكُمْ ۚ إِنَّ الَّذِينَ يَسْتَكْبِرُونَ عَنْ عِبَادَتِي سَيَدْخُلُونَ جَهَنَّمَ دَاخِرِينَ

'Your Lord has proclaimed, "Call upon Me, I will respond to you. Surely those who are too proud to worship Me will enter Hell, fully humbled."' (40:60)

"Notice," he continued, "this isn't a conditional promise. Allah doesn't say 'I might respond' or 'I'll respond if certain conditions are met.' He simply says, 'I will respond.' This is a divine guarantee from the One who never breaks His promises."

Sara wiped her tears. "But then why haven't I gotten into medical school? I've been making du'aa for years."

Her uncle smiled gently. "Perhaps we need to understand what 'response' really means in Allah's wisdom."

The Divine Guarantee

The promise of Allah to answer our prayers represents one of the most intimate and powerful connections we have with our Creator. It appears in multiple places throughout the Qur'an, emphasizing its importance in our relationship with Allah.

In Surat Al-Baqarah, Allah elaborates on this promise with beautiful reassurance:

وَإِذَا سَأَلَكَ عِبَادِي عَنِّي فَإِنِّي قَرِيبٌ ۖ أُجِيبُ دَعْوَةَ الدَّاعِ إِذَا دَعَانِ ۖ فَلْيَسْتَجِيبُوا لِي وَلْيُؤْمِنُوا بِي لَعَلَّهُمْ يَرْشُدُونَ

"When My servants ask you ˹O Prophet˺ about Me: I am truly near. I respond to one's prayer when they call upon Me. So let them respond ˹with obedience˺ to Me and believe in Me, perhaps they will be guided ˹to the Right Way˺." (2:186)

Notice the immediate reassurance: "I am truly near." Before even mentioning the response to prayer, Allah addresses our deepest fear, that He might be distant or unaware of our situation. By affirming His nearness first, He soothes the anxious heart that wonders if its prayers are even being heard.

Three Ways Allah ﷻ Responds

To understand the depth of Allah's promise regarding du'aa, we must recognize that divine responses come in various forms, all representing perfect wisdom.

The Prophet ﷺ explained this comprehensively:

> "There is no Muslim who calls upon Allah, without sin or cutting family ties, but that Allah will give him one of three answers: He will quickly fulfill his supplication, He will store it for him in the Hereafter, or He will divert an evil from him similar to it." They said, "In that case, we will ask for more." The Prophet said, "Allah has even more."[30]

This hadith reveals a profound truth: every good du'aa is answered, without exception. The form of the answer, however, falls into at least one of three categories:

1. Immediate fulfillment - Receiving exactly what we asked for in this life
2. Stored for the Hereafter - Receiving something far better in the eternal life to come
3. Averting an equivalent harm - Being protected from a calamity we weren't even aware of

Let's explore how these divine responses manifest in our lives.

The Unexpected Job Offer: When Du'aa is Fulfilled Immediately

Salman, a father of three, lost his job during a major economic downturn. Week after week, he submitted applications without receiving any responses. Each night, he would pray the tahajjud prayer, asking Allah for provision for his family.

"One particular night remains etched in my memory," Salman recalled. "I felt a special connection during my du'aa, crying as I asked Allah to open a door of provision. The very next morning, I received a call from a company I hadn't even applied to. A former colleague had recommended me for a position I didn't know existed."

The new position offered better compensation and working conditions than Salman's previous job. "The timing was so precise that I couldn't attribute it to coincidence," he explained. "It was a direct, immediate response to my du'aa that came through a channel I never anticipated."

This represents the first type of response mentioned in the hadith—immediate fulfillment. Sometimes Allah ﷻ answers exactly as we ask, when the request aligns with His wisdom and our ultimate benefit.

The Story of Umm Salamah

The beautiful story of Umm Salamah illustrates how Allah ﷻ sometimes responds with something far better than what we initially request.

After the death of her beloved husband Abu Salamah, Umm Salamah was devastated. She recalled that the Prophet Muhammad ﷺ had taught believers to say during calamity:

إِنَّا لِلَّهِ وَإِنَّا إِلَيْهِ رَاجِعُونَ، اللَّهُمَّ أْجُرْنِي فِي مُصِيبَتِي وَأَخْلِفْ لِي خَيْرًا مِنْهَا

"We belong to Allah, and to Him we shall return. O Allah, reward me for my affliction and replace it with something better."

Umm Salamah (ra) recited this du'aa faithfully, but then thought to herself, "Who could be better than Abu Salamah?" She couldn't imagine anyone who could replace her husband.

Yet Allah ﷻ had planned something extraordinary. After her period of mourning (iddah) ended, the Prophet Muhammad ﷺ himself proposed marriage to her. Umm Salamah, who had been a widow worried about raising her children alone, became a Mother of the Believers, married to the best of creation ﷺ.

When she reflected on her seemingly impossible du'aa, Umm Salamah realized that Allah had indeed given her something far better than she could have imagined. Her story teaches us that sometimes when we think our prayers aren't being answered, Allah is actually preparing something superior to what we requested.

Protection Through Rejected Requests: Ayman's Story

Ayman's story illustrates the third type of response, when Allah protects us by not giving us what we ask for.

A talented software engineer, Ayman had set his heart on a prestigious position with a tech giant in another country. The salary was exceptional, the benefits impressive, and the status would fulfill his lifelong ambition. He made du'aa constantly, asking Allah to grant him this opportunity.

After reaching the final round of interviews, Ayman was rejected. "I was devastated," he admitted. "I questioned everything, my abilities, my worth, and even my faith. Why would Allah deny me something so perfect?"

Six months later, the company made headlines for all the wrong reasons. A major scandal revealed toxic working conditions, and hundreds of employees in Ayman's potential department were laid off. Many who had relocated their families found themselves stranded in an expensive foreign country without income.

"Looking back, I realized that what I perceived as rejection was actually protection," Ayman reflected. "Allah ﷻ knew what I couldn't see, that this 'dream job' would have led to tremendous stress, possible unemployment, and being far from my support network during a crisis." This represents the third type of response in the Prophet's ﷺ hadith, averting an equivalent harm. Sometimes Allah's "no" is actually the most merciful response possible.

When Du'aa Redirects Our Path

Three months later, Sara received an unexpected offer to work as a research assistant at a medical institution. Though it wasn't medical school, she was learning medicine from a different angle. Her work led to significant contributions and a co-authored research paper.

"When I reapplied, I was accepted to three schools," Sara shared. "But I realized I loved research more than clinical practice. I ended up pursuing a Ph.D. instead. Allah answered my prayer by showing me a better path I hadn't considered."

Enhancing Our Du'aa

Given Allah's guaranteed response, how can we optimize our approach to du'aa? The Prophet ﷺ taught us several principles:

1. Begin with praise of Allah and sending blessings upon the Prophet ﷺ

The Prophet ﷺ once heard a man making du'aa without praising Allah ﷻ or sending blessings upon him. He commented: "This one has rushed."[31] He then taught that proper du'aa begins with praising Allah and sending blessings upon the Prophet ﷺ before making requests.

2. Raise your hands

The Prophet ﷺ said: "Indeed, Allah is conscientious and generous. He would be shy, when a man (or woman) raises his hands to Him, to turn them away empty and disappointed."[32]

3. Make du'aa with certainty and conviction

The Prophet ﷺ advised: "Call upon Allah with certainty that He will answer you, and know that Allah does not respond to a supplication from a negligent, inattentive heart."[33]

4. Persist without giving up

The Prophet ﷺ emphasized persistence: "Your du'aa will be answered as long as you don't grow impatient saying: 'I made du'aa but received no response.'"[34]

Du'aa as Worship: Beyond Just Asking

Imam Ahmad b. Ḥanbal beautifully captured the essence of du'aa in his own supplication: "O Allah, just as You have protected my face from prostrating to other than You, then protect it from asking other than You."[35]

This profound statement reminds us that du'aa is not merely a transactional request for needs, it is an act of worship that affirms our complete dependence on Allah and our recognition of His unlimited power.

The Prophet ﷺ explicitly stated: "Du'aa is worship."[36] This perspective transforms our understanding of du'aa. Even when we don't receive exactly what we asked for, the very act of turning to Allah in supplication fulfills the primary purpose, establishing and strengthening our connection with our Creator.

Du'aa in Times of Ease and Hardship

The Prophet ﷺ said: "Whoever wishes that Allah would respond to him during hardship and distress, then let him make plenty of du'aa in times of ease."[37] This teaching encourages us to establish a consistent practice of du'aa during good times, not just when we're desperate. Khalid, a community leader, shared how this principle transformed his relationship with du'aa: "I used to mainly make du'aa when I needed something urgently," he admitted. "Then I started dedicating a few minutes after each prayer to sincerely thank Allah and make du'aa, even when life was good and I didn't have pressing needs."

When Khalid later faced a serious family crisis, he found that turning to Allah in du'aa felt natural and comforting. "Because I had established that connection during easy times, I felt Allah's nearness during my hardship. The response to my prayers came with a peace I hadn't experienced before."

Special Times and Places for Du'aa

While Allah accepts du'aa at all times, the Prophet ﷺ informed us of certain moments when acceptance is especially likely, such as:

1. During the last third of the night
The Prophet ﷺ said: "Our Lord ﷻ descends to the lowest heaven during the last third of the night and says: 'Who is calling upon Me so that I may answer him? Who is asking from Me so that I may give him? Who is seeking My forgiveness so that I may forgive him?'"[38]

2. Between the adhan and iqāmah
The Prophet ﷺ said: "Du'aa made between the adhān and iqāmah is not rejected."[39]

3. During prostration
The Prophet ﷺ advised: "The closest a servant is to his Lord is when he is in prostration, so make plenty of du'aa then."[40]

4. On the Day of 'Arafah
The Prophet ﷺ said: "The best supplication is the supplication on the Day of 'Arafah."[41]

5. During the rain
The Prophet ﷺ said: "Two (du'aas) are not rejected: du'aa at the time of the call to prayer and du'a at the time of rain."[42]

Knowing these special times (and others) can help us optimize our du'aa practice, but they should not limit us, Allah hears our supplications at all times.

Du'aa That Changed History

Throughout Islamic history, we find remarkable examples of du'aa changing seemingly impossible situations. Prophet Ayyub, after years of illness and loss, made a simple but profound du'aa:

أَنِّي مَسَّنِيَ الضُّرُّ وَأَنتَ أَرْحَمُ الرَّاحِمِينَ

"Indeed, adversity has touched me, and You are the Most Merciful of the merciful." (21:83)

Allah ﷻ responded immediately:

فَاسْتَجَبْنَا لَهُ فَكَشَفْنَا مَا بِهِ مِن ضُرٍّ

"So We responded to him and removed the adversity that was upon him." (21:84)

When Du'aa Seems Delayed

If we feel our du'aa remains unanswered, the Prophet Muhammad ﷺ encouraged us to look inward. Sa'd ibn Abi Waqqās (ra) reported that the Prophet ﷺ said: "Indeed, Allah is Pure and only accepts what is pure."[43]

This might lead us to examine:

1. Is our income and food from pure (halal) sources?
2. Are we making du'aa while engaged in sin without sincere repentance?
3. Are we asking for something harmful without realizing it?
4. Have we become impatient and given up on repeated du'aa?

The Prophet ﷺ said: "The du'aa of any one of you will be answered so long as he does not seek to hasten it and does not pray for something sinful or for breaking family ties."[44]

The Promise That Never Fails

My dear brothers and sisters, as we navigate the complexities and challenges of modern life, Allah's promise to answer our du'aa stands as a pillar of hope and reassurance.

No matter how difficult our circumstances, how overwhelming our problems, or how distant our goals may seem, we have direct access to the Creator of the universe who has guaranteed His response.

When we truly internalize this divine promise, our perspective on life's challenges transforms. Difficulties become opportunities to witness Allah's intervention. Delayed dreams become invitations to trust His perfect timing. Even apparent rejections become expressions of His protection and wisdom.

Let us remember the beautiful words of our Lord:

وَقَالَ رَبُّكُمُ ادْعُونِي أَسْتَجِبْ لَكُمْ

"Your Lord has proclaimed, 'Call upon Me, I will respond to you.'" (40:60)

This is a direct invitation from the Creator, a divine guarantee establishing the most intimate connection possible between us and our Lord.

Every sincere du'aa receives a response: immediate fulfillment, reward in the Hereafter, or protection from unseen harm. Let us make du'aa with conviction and trust, knowing that the One who created us knows exactly what we need and when we need it.

Discussion Questions

1. Think of a time when you felt your du'aa wasn't answered, only to later realize it was answered in a better way. How did this experience change your understanding of Allah's wisdom?
2. How might knowing that every sincere du'aa receives one of three responses (immediate fulfillment, reward in the Hereafter, or averting harm) change your approach to making du'aa? Does this knowledge provide comfort during times when you don't see an immediate response?
3. The chapter mentions several times and conditions when du'aa is especially likely to be accepted (like during prostration or the last third of the night). Which of these special times could you realistically incorporate into your regular practice, and what practical steps would you need to take to do so?

"O Allah, I ask You for Your grace and mercy, for no one possesses them except You. O Allah, the Ever-Living, the Self-Sustaining, forgive us and accept from us."

11

The Promise of Divine Support

Paris, France

The evening prayer had just concluded at the university mosque when Tariq, a second-year engineering student, approached Imam Majed with a troubled expression.

"What's on your mind, my young brother?" the imam asked gently.

"I'm feeling... overwhelmed," Tariq admitted. "In class today, when I excused myself for Ẓuhr prayer, my professor made some dismissive comments about 'religious obligations interfering with education.' Some students laughed. I felt humiliated and, honestly, abandoned."

The imam nodded thoughtfully. "Did you complete your prayer anyway?"

"Yes," Tariq replied. "But I felt alone. Where was Allah's support when I was being mocked for obeying Him?"

Imam Majed compassionately responded, "Let me share something with you that changed my understanding of divine support forever." He recited:

يَا أَيُّهَا الَّذِينَ آمَنُوا إِن تَنصُرُوا اللَّهَ يَنصُرْكُمْ وَيُثَبِّتْ أَقْدَامَكُمْ

"Believers, if you aid Allah, He will come to your aid and will plant your feet firmly." (47:7)

Tariq listened attentively as the imam continued, "Notice the sequence here, our support for Allah's cause comes first, then His support follows. What you experienced today was not abandonment; it was an opportunity. By maintaining your prayer despite mockery, you were supporting Allah's cause. Now watch how His support manifests in your life."

A month later, Tariq returned to the imam with a different expression altogether. "Something remarkable happened," he began. "After that day, I continued praying on time, despite the professor's disapproval. Then last week, he called me to his office. I expected more criticism, but instead, he apologized. He said he'd been reflecting on his behavior and realized he wasn't upholding the university's commitment to religious diversity. But here's what's truly amazing, he asked me about Islam. We had a thirty-minute conversation about faith and science. He's even considering allowing a formal prayer break for all students with religious obligations."

The imam smiled. "Allah's support often comes in ways we never expect. You stood firm for Him, and look how He planted your feet firmly and turned a challenge into an opportunity for da'wah. Just remember, even if your professor continued to insult you or harass you, just as all the prophets and messengers faced harassment, it doesn't mean that Allah isn't giving you a divine support in other ways that you might not detect. In fact, your very consistency in prayer and firmness in the obligation is a beautiful sign of that divine aid."

A Two-Way Relationship

The divine promise contained in Surat Muhammad establishes one of the most powerful principles in our relationship with Allah, that divine support operates as a two-way commitment. This verse appears after one of the 89 instances in the Qur'an where Allah addresses believers directly with "O you who believe," signaling the exceptional importance of what follows.

The promise is both straightforward and profound: when we support Allah's cause, He supports us and plants our feet firmly. This creates a dynamic relationship where our sincere efforts activate divine assistance in our lives.

What Does It Mean to "Support Allah?"

The concept of "supporting Allah" might seem puzzling. After all, Allah describes Himself as Al-Ghaniyy (The Self-Sufficient). Thus, how can the Creator of the universe, who needs nothing from His creation, require our "support?" The answer lies in understanding what "supporting Allah" truly means. It isn't about Allah needing our help, but rather about us aligning ourselves with divine purpose.

When we support Allah's cause:

1. We fulfill our purpose as khalifah (vicegerents) on earth
2. We become vessels through which divine guidance reaches others
3. We align our will with Allah's will, creating harmony in our existence
4. We participate in the establishment of justice and goodness in the world

The Hospital Director's Choice

Dr. Khan, newly appointed hospital director, faced immediate pressure to convert the prayer room into storage because of an urgent situation with construction. Despite risks to her credibility, she prepared a proposal showing how proper prayer facilities would benefit staff wellbeing and patient care.

"The board meeting was tense," she recalled. "Some implied I was pushing a 'religious agenda.'" Yet non-Muslim board members supported religious accommodation as workplace diversity. The proposal passed.

The new prayer facility improved staff retention and fostered interfaith dialogue. "By standing for Allah's cause professionally, I witnessed His support in unexpected ways," Dr. Khan reflected. "My position wasn't weakened, it was strengthened."

Four Pillars of Supporting Allah's Cause

Supporting Allah's cause isn't limited to grand gestures or public advocacy. It manifests in daily choices that collectively shape our relationship with our Creator and His creation. Based on the teachings of the Qur'an and Sunnah, we can identify four fundamental pillars of supporting Allah's cause:

1. Prioritizing Divine Revelation in Our Decisions

In our own lives, prioritizing divine revelation means consulting the Qur'an and authentic Sunnah when making significant decisions, seeking knowledge to understand them correctly, and valuing Islamic principles even when they conflict with our desires or cultural norms.

2. Implementing Islamic Commandments Consistently

Supporting Allah's cause requires moving beyond intellectual acknowledgment to consistent implementation of Islamic teachings. This might mean:

- Structuring our financial dealings to avoid interest (ribā)
- Observing the Islamic dress code despite social pressure
- Maintaining prayer times even when inconvenient
- Fasting Ramadan while managing professional obligations
- Giving zakat and charity despite economic concerns

3. Actively Promoting Good and Preventing Harm

The Prophet ﷺ taught: "Whoever among you sees evil, let him change it with his hand. If he is unable to do so, then with his tongue. If he is unable to do so, then with his heart, and that is the weakest of faith."[45]

4. Standing Firm in Defense of Truth and Justice

Allah repeatedly emphasizes the importance of standing for justice, even when difficult:

يَا أَيُّهَا الَّذِينَ آمَنُوا كُونُوا قَوَّامِينَ بِالْقِسْطِ شُهَدَاءَ لِلَّهِ وَلَوْ عَلَىٰ أَنفُسِكُمْ أَوِ الْوَالِدَيْنِ وَالْأَقْرَبِينَ

"O believers! Stand firm for justice as witnesses for Allah even if it is against yourselves, your parents, or close relatives." (4:135)

Omar, a lawyer working for a major American corporation, discovered that his company was involved in practices that harmed vulnerable communities. Despite the risk to his career, he documented the issues and advocated for change internally. When the company resisted, he resigned and helped those affected seek justice.

"It was the most difficult decision of my career," Omar admitted. "I had monthly house payments, family responsibilities, and no immediate job prospects. But I couldn't reconcile supporting injustice with my identity as a Muslim."

Within months, Omar received an unexpected job offer from a firm specializing in corporate ethics, with better compensation and alignment with his values. "Allah's support came in a form I never anticipated," he reflected. "What seemed like career suicide became the path to more meaningful work."

Beyond Military Victory

Salahuddin's greatness wasn't just liberating Al-Aqsa (Jerusalem) but upholding Islamic principles even in warfare. Despite Crusader brutality, he forbade revenge against civilians when recapturing the city. As is well documented even by Christian historians, when Christians took Jerusalem, they filled it with Muslim blood. When Salahuddin retook it, he forbade killing Christians and allowed safe passage. This wasn't strategy, it reflected understanding that supporting Allah's cause meant embodying justice and mercy regardless of circumstances.

Divine Support in Action

When we fulfill our part by supporting Allah's cause, His support manifests in multiple dimensions:

1. Internal Strength and Conviction

Allah ﷻ affirms this internal support:

هُوَ الَّذِي أَنزَلَ السَّكِينَةَ فِي قُلُوبِ الْمُؤْمِنِينَ لِيَزْدَادُوا إِيمَانًا مَّعَ إِيمَانِهِمْ

"He is the One Who sent down tranquility into the hearts of the believers so that they would increase in faith along with their [present] faith." (48:4)

With each challenge faced for Allah's sake, conviction deepens rather than weakens.

2. Guidance in Difficult Decisions

وَمَن يَتَّقِ اللَّهَ يَجْعَل لَّهُ مَخْرَجًا وَيَرْزُقْهُ مِنْ حَيْثُ لَا يَحْتَسِبُ

"And whoever fears Allah, He will make for him a way out and will provide for him from where he does not expect." (65:2-3)

Doors close to harmful opportunities while better paths open.

3. Protection from Harm
Allah ﷻ promises this protection:

إِنَّ اللَّهَ يُدَافِعُ عَنِ الَّذِينَ آمَنُوا

"Indeed, Allah defends those who believe." (22:38)

What seems like missing out becomes comprehensive protection.

4. Peace of Heart and Mind
Perhaps the most immediate form of divine support is the profound inner peace that comes from aligning with Allah's will. This serenity isn't circumstantial, it is Allah's gift of 'sakīnah' (tranquility) that He promises to those who prioritize His pleasure over worldly gain.

Beginning Your Journey

Supporting Allah's cause begins with small but consistent actions that gradually transform our relationship with our Creator and His creation:

1. Stand firm in your daily prayers despite busy schedules. Allah ﷻ reminds us:

حَافِظُوا عَلَى الصَّلَوَاتِ وَالصَّلَاةِ الْوُسْطَىٰ وَقُومُوا لِلَّهِ قَانِتِينَ

"Maintain with care the [obligatory] prayers and [in particular] the middle [i.e., 'asr] prayer and stand before Allah, devoutly obedient." (2:238)

When we prioritize prayer, even rearranging meetings, pausing entertainment, or momentarily stepping away from social gatherings, we actively demonstrate that Allah's commands take precedence in our lives.

2. Speak truth even when uncomfortable.
This might mean correcting misinformation about Islam, standing up for someone being treated unjustly, or simply refusing to participate in backbiting or gossip. Each instance of speaking truth supports Allah's cause.

3. Maintain Islamic ethics in business dealings
The Prophet ﷺ said: "The merchants will be raised on the Day of Resurrection as wicked, except for those who fear Allah, are righteous, and are truthful."[46] In

practical terms, this includes transparent pricing, honest marketing, fair treatment of employees, and avoiding prohibited transactions regardless of potential profit.

4. Support justice and oppose oppression within our sphere of influence
The Prophet ﷺ said: "Help your brother, whether he is an oppressor or is oppressed." When asked how to help an oppressor, he clarified: "By preventing him from oppressing others."[47] This might include advocating for fair workplace policies, supporting ethical sourcing of products, or simply intervening when someone is being mistreated.

5. Teach others about Islam through character and actions
The Prophet ﷺ was described as a "walking Qur'an," embodying the values he taught.[48] When we consistently demonstrate Islamic virtues like honesty, compassion, excellence, and trustworthiness, we support Allah's cause by making His guidance visible and attractive to others.

The Promise That Strengthens Us

My dear brothers and sisters, as we navigate the complexities of modern life, with its competing priorities, ethical dilemmas, and social pressures, Allah's promise of support stands as an unwavering source of strength and guidance:

يَا أَيُّهَا الَّذِينَ آمَنُوا إِن تَنصُرُوا اللَّهَ يَنصُرْكُمْ وَيُثَبِّتْ أَقْدَامَكُمْ

"Believers, if you aid Allah, He will come to your aid and will plant your feet firmly." (47:7)

This divine guarantee transforms how we approach challenges. We no longer face them alone, armed only with our limited capabilities. Instead, we face them with the certainty that the Creator of the universe has promised His support when we align ourselves with His cause.

In an age where Muslims often feel marginalized, this promise reminds us that divine support doesn't depend on our numbers, resources, or worldly power. It depends solely on our commitment to supporting Allah's cause through consistent obedience and steadfast principles.

Let us move forward with renewed commitment in every aspect, personal habits, family dynamics, professional environments, and community engagement. As we do, we'll witness firsthand: He will support us and plant our feet firmly on the path of truth, justice, and eternal success.

Discussion Questions

1. In what specific ways can you "support Allah's cause" in your daily life and professional environment? Identify one area where you could take a more active stance in upholding Islamic principles, and what practical steps would this involve?
2. How does understanding that Allah is Al-Ghaniyy (Self-Sufficient) change your perspective on what it means to "support" His cause? In what ways does this understanding liberate you from focusing on results and redirect your attention to sincerity of effort?
3. Looking at the examples of historical Muslim figures mentioned in this chapter, what qualities and actions made them successful in supporting Allah's cause, and how can you emulate these qualities in your contemporary context? Which of their characteristics do you find most inspiring and relevant to your own situation?

"Our Lord, pour upon us patience and plant our feet firmly and give us victory over the disbelieving people."

12

The Promise That Charity Will Be Replaced

London, England

The fundraising event for the new Islamic center had nearly reached its conclusion. As the imam announced they were still $50,000 short of their goal, an uncomfortable silence fell over the hall. It was then that Waleed, a local businessman who had already contributed generously, stood up.

"I'll pledge the remaining $50,000," he announced, his voice steady despite the significant commitment he had just made.

Later, as people thanked him for his generosity, a young man approached Waleed with genuine curiosity. "Weren't you worried about making such a large donation?" he asked. "That's a substantial amount to part with."

Waleed smiled. "Three years ago, I was hesitant to give even a fraction of that amount. Then I came across a verse that transformed my relationship with wealth forever. Allah promises:

قُلْ إِنَّ رَبِّي يَبْسُطُ الرِّزْقَ لِمَن يَشَاءُ مِنْ عِبَادِهِ وَيَقْدِرُ لَهُ ۚ وَمَا أَنفَقْتُم مِّن شَيْءٍ فَهُوَ يُخْلِفُهُ ۖ وَهُوَ خَيْرُ الرَّازِقِينَ

"Say, ˹O Prophet,˺ Surely ˹it is˺ my Lord ˹Who˺ gives abundant or limited provisions to whoever He wills of His servants. And whatever you spend in charity, He will compensate ˹you˺ for it. For He is the Best Provider." (34:39)

"When I truly internalized this verse," Waleed continued, "I decided to fully lean on Allah's promise. I made a significant donation during a previous fundraiser, an amount that frankly made me nervous. Within six months, my business secured contracts that brought in tenfold what I had given. It wasn't just financial return; I experienced a profound sense of barakah in all aspects of my life."

He placed his hand gently on the young man's shoulder. "The more I give, the more I witness Allah's promise fulfilled in ways I could never have anticipated. It's not about the math, it's about trusting the One who owns everything."

The young man nodded thoughtfully. "I appreciate your perspective, but my situation is quite different. I'm a student with barely enough to cover my expenses. The twenty dollars I donated tonight was actually my food money for next week. Does such a small amount even matter in the grand scheme?"

Waleed's eyes lit up. "Brother, your twenty dollars may well be more significant than my fifty thousand! Let me share with you a beautiful hadith. The Prophet ﷺ said, "A dirham surpassed a hundred thousand dirhams."

When his companions asked how this could be possible, he explained: "A man had two dirhams; he gave one in charity. Another man had a great amount of wealth; he took out a hundred thousand dirhams and gave them in charity."[49]

This hadith brilliantly reframes our understanding of generosity. In Allah's divine economy, the value of charity isn't measured by the absolute amount given but by the proportion it represents of what we possess and the sacrifice it entails.

The man who gave one dirham sacrificed 50% of his worldly wealth, while the one who gave a hundred thousand dirhams might have parted with just 1% or even 0.1% of his fortune. Though the wealthy man's contribution was objectively larger and he will be immensely rewarded, the poor man's sacrifice was proportionally greater and more difficult.

There are hundreds of similar stories to great provision following difficult charities. In Michigan, a student named Omar gave all his wealth, $50, because of how motivated he was in the promise of Allah. He swore that the next Monday morning, he received an unexpected email related to an application he submitted months earlier. He received a scholarship that was highly competitive, and it was for $2500! He cried when he read the email in disbelief and shared his story in the hopes of motivating others.

The Value of Sacrifice in Charity

Allah ﷻ tells us:

لَن تَنَالُوا الْبِرَّ حَتَّىٰ تُنفِقُوا مِمَّا تُحِبُّونَ

"You will not attain righteousness until you spend from that which you love." (3:92)

Meaningful charity involves some level of sacrifice, giving from what we value, not merely from our excess. When we part with something dear to us for Allah's sake, we demonstrate a prioritization of eternal values over temporary possessions.

This principle plays out differently in each person's life. For someone of modest means, giving fifty dollars might represent a significant sacrifice. For a wealthy individual, a much larger amount might be needed to achieve the same level of meaningful giving. Allah, in His perfect wisdom, evaluates charity by what it represents to the giver, not by its objective monetary value.

Overcoming the Whispers of Fear

Despite the clear divine promise of compensation, many of us hesitate to give generously. What holds us back? Often, it's the whisper of fear that Shaytān plants in our hearts:

الشَّيْطَانُ يَعِدُكُمُ الْفَقْرَ وَيَأْمُرُكُم بِالْفَحْشَاءِ

"Satan threatens you with poverty and orders you to immorality." (2:268)

Talia, a single mother, confronted this fear when considering sponsoring an orphan. Despite doubts, she signed up. Within weeks, she received an unexpected promotion that more than covered her charity. "The fear never completely disappears," she shared, "but each time I give despite it, my trust grows stronger."

Divine Mathematics

While Allah promises to replace what we spend in charity, numerous verses suggest that the compensation often exceeds the original amount many times over:

مَّثَلُ الَّذِينَ يُنفِقُونَ أَمْوَالَهُمْ فِي سَبِيلِ اللَّهِ كَمَثَلِ حَبَّةٍ أَنبَتَتْ سَبْعَ سَنَابِلَ فِي كُلِّ سُنبُلَةٍ مِّائَةُ حَبَّةٍ ۗ
وَاللَّهُ يُضَاعِفُ لِمَن يَشَاءُ ۗ وَاللَّهُ وَاسِعٌ عَلِيمٌ

"The example of those who spend their wealth in the way of Allah is like a seed that grows seven spikes; in each spike is a hundred grains. And Allah multiplies [His reward] for whom He wills. And Allah is all-Encompassing and Knowing." (2:261)

This verse presents a mathematical multiplication that defies conventional economics, one seed producing seven hundred grains, representing a 700-fold return. Even more remarkably, the verse adds that "Allah multiplies for whom He wills," suggesting that the return can be even greater.

Mu'adh witnessed this when he donated $10,000 that he'd saved for his daughter's education during a flood crisis. Years later, his daughter received a full scholarship worth $120,000. "I gave $10,000 and Allah returned it twelve-fold," he reflected.

What some Muslims oftentimes forget is that the promise is not about multiplying one's wealth immediately, or in a manner that is obvious. The promise may bring other types of blessings in this world, or protection against severe harm, all with a promise of multiplied rewards in the afterlife that will shade the believer and intercede for them as their ranks in paradise increase.

The Prophetic Model

Our beloved Prophet Muhammad ﷺ exemplified fearless generosity in ways that continue to inspire believers fourteen centuries later: "The Messenger of Allah was the most generous of people, and he was most generous during Ramadan when Jibreel would meet him."[50] Another beautiful description states: "The Prophet ﷺ was more generous with good than the sent wind."[51]

This poetic comparison to the "sent wind" (الرِّيحِ الْمُرْسَلَةِ) is particularly meaningful. Wind brings rain that revives the earth, spreads seeds that produce harvest, and reaches everyone without discrimination. Similarly, the Prophet's generosity was:

1. Revitalizing – bringing life to those in need
2. Productive – creating ongoing benefit
3. Universal – extending to all, regardless of status
4. Consistent – like the natural cycles of wind and rain

Perhaps most remarkably, this generosity persisted even when the Prophet ﷺ himself had limited resources. Anas ibn Malik (ra) reported: "The Messenger of Allah was never asked for anything upon Islam but that he gave it."[52]

Forms of Divine Compensation

While we often think of compensation for charity in purely financial terms, Allah's replacement often comes in diverse and unexpected forms:

1. Barakah in What Remains. The Prophet ﷺ said: "Charity never decreases wealth."[53] This seemingly paradoxical statement points to the concept of barakah, divine blessing that causes what remains to stretch further, satisfy more deeply, and fulfill needs more completely.
2. Protection from Harm. The Prophet ﷺ advised: "Treat your sick by giving charity."[54] This indicates that charity can serve as a spiritual protection against calamities and illness.
3. Spiritual Growth and Peace. Beyond material compensation, charity nurtures spiritual development and inner peace.

Maximizing the Divine Promise

To fully experience the promise of divine compensation, consider these principles drawn from Islamic teachings:

1. Give from the Best of What You Have

وَلَا تَيَمَّمُوا الْخَبِيثَ مِنْهُ تُنفِقُونَ

"And do not aim toward the defective therefrom, spending [from that]." (2:267)

Practically, this means giving from our quality possessions, preferred income sources, and prime time, not just what we don't want or can easily spare.

2. Give Consistently, Even If Small
The Prophet ﷺ taught: "The most beloved deeds to Allah are those that are most consistent, even if small."[55]

Regular, sustainable giving often carries more spiritual benefit than occasional large donations. Setting up automatic monthly charitable contributions, even if modest, embodies this principle.

3. Give Discreetly When Possible
Allah praises those who give secretly:

إِن تُبْدُوا الصَّدَقَاتِ فَنِعِمَّا هِيَ ۖ وَإِن تُخْفُوهَا وَتُؤْتُوهَا الْفُقَرَاءَ فَهُوَ خَيْرٌ لَّكُمْ

"If you disclose your charitable expenditures, they are good; but if you conceal them and give them to the poor, it is better for you." (2:271)

While public charity has its place (especially in encouraging others), private giving protects our intention and often carries special blessing.

4. Give in Times of Both Ease and Hardship

الَّذِينَ يُنفِقُونَ فِي السَّرَّاءِ وَالضَّرَّاءِ

"Those who spend [in the cause of Allah] during ease and hardship." (3:134)

Maintaining charitable giving even during personal financial challenges demonstrates profound trust in Allah's promise of compensation.

The Promise That Transforms

Allah's promise to replace what we spend in charity fundamentally transforms our relationship with wealth. Rather than seeing our resources as limited assets to be carefully guarded, we recognize them as channels through which Allah's provision flows. When we give, we aren't diminishing our resources, we're creating space for Allah to replenish them, often in greater measure. This isn't prosperity gospel or materialistic thinking; it's taking Allah at His word when He promises:

وَمَا أَنفَقْتُم مِّن شَيْءٍ فَهُوَ يُخْلِفُهُ

"And whatever you spend in charity, He will compensate ⌜you⌝ for it." (34:39)

The Prophet ﷺ said: "Allah says: 'Spend, O son of Adam, and I shall spend on you'"[56] This divine statement perfectly encapsulates the flowing, reciprocal nature of true charity. Our giving doesn't occur in a closed system where resources are finite. Rather, it connects us to the infinite treasury of the Most Generous.

Each act of charity offers an opportunity to strengthen our trust. Start where you are, with what you can sincerely offer. The compensation may come swiftly or gradually, in expected or surprising forms. But it will come, for Allah never fails in His promise.

Beyond material replacement lies something more valuable, the spiritual wealth of participating in the divine economy of generosity, where nothing given is ever lost, and everything shared returns multiplied.

Discussion Questions

1. How does the story of the man who gave one dirham reshape your understanding of generosity and sacrifice? Think about a time when you gave a relatively small amount that was actually significant from your personal perspective.
2. In what ways can we overcome the fear of poverty when it comes to giving in charity? Which of Allah's promises about provision most resonates with you personally?
3. Reflect on a personal experience where giving in charity led to unexpected blessings. How did this experience affect your trust in Allah's promise of compensation?

"O Allah, give compensation to the one who gives charity, make us generous and not stingy, and bless us in our provisions."

13

The Promise of a Good Life

Sydney, Australia

The small apartment was sparsely furnished but immaculately clean. Sunlight streamed through the simple curtains, illuminating the face of Maya as she poured tea for her visitor, a young doctoral student researching "happiness across socioeconomic levels" for her psychology dissertation.

"I've interviewed dozens of people in upscale neighborhoods," the student explained, "and now I'm gathering perspectives from—" she hesitated, searching for a tactful phrase.

"From the poor?" Maya smiled gently. "There's no shame in acknowledging my financial situation, my daughter."

The student nodded, slightly embarrassed. "I've found that many wealthy people I've interviewed express significant dissatisfaction despite their abundance. I'm curious about your perspective on happiness given your... different circumstances."

Maya's eyes crinkled as she smiled. "Let me tell you about two women I know," she began. "The first lives in a luxurious home with every modern convenience. Her closets overflow with designer clothes, many still bearing their tags. Her kitchen boasts appliances she's never used. Yet she constantly compares herself to others who have more and feels her life is lacking.

"The second woman lives simply, owning just what she needs. Her modest home is filled with laughter and remembrance of Allah. When she receives something new, she expresses genuine gratitude. She sleeps peacefully, trusting that tomorrow's provision is in Allah's hands."

"They sound very different," the student remarked, jotting notes. "Who are these women?"

Maya's eyes twinkled. "The second woman is me. The first was also me, twenty years ago, before I found the true meaning of a good life."

The student looked up, confused. "You were wealthy before?"

"I had a high-paying corporate position, a luxury apartment, and all the trappings of success," Maya explained. "But I was constantly anxious, always striving for more, never satisfied. Then I discovered a profound promise in the Qur'an that transformed my understanding of what makes life truly good. Allah tells us:

مَنْ عَمِلَ صَالِحًا مِّن ذَكَرٍ أَوْ أُنثَىٰ وَهُوَ مُؤْمِنٌ فَلَنُحْيِيَنَّهُۥ حَيَاةً طَيِّبَةً ۖ وَلَنَجْزِيَنَّهُمْ أَجْرَهُم بِأَحْسَنِ مَا كَانُوا۟ يَعْمَلُونَ

"Whoever does good, whether male or female, and is a believer, We will surely bless them with a good life, and We will certainly reward them according to the best of their deeds." (16:97)

"This verse," Maya continued, her voice soft with reverence, "contains a divine promise of a 'ḥayātan ṭayyibah—a good, pure, wholesome life. But notice the conditions: righteous deeds and faith. The quality of life that Allah promises isn't measured by wealth or status but by inward contentment and meaningful living. It doesn't mean you choose poverty, but rather you control wealth in your hands and not your heart; now I invest it in foundations and organizations that do meaningful work instead of just buying unnecessary status symbols."

The student looked around the modest apartment with new eyes, suddenly aware of something she hadn't noticed before, a profound sense of peace that permeated the space.

"So you're saying you're happier now with less?"

"I'm saying I discovered what 'more' truly means," Maya replied. "And it wasn't what I thought."

Understanding the Divine Promise

The promise contained in verse 16:97 of the Qur'an offers a revolutionary perspective on what constitutes a good life. In a world fixated on material prosperity as the primary measure of success, Allah presents a different equation:

Righteous Deeds + Faith = Ḥayātan Ṭayyibah (A Good Life)

Several aspects of this divine promise deserve our careful attention:

1. It's gender-inclusive: The phrase "whether male or female" emphasizes that this good life is accessible to all believers regardless of gender.
2. It requires both faith and action: The twin conditions of belief (īmān) and righteous deeds ('amal ṣāliḥ) indicate that faith without action, or action without faith, is insufficient.
3. It's a divine guarantee: The Arabic construction using "la" (لَ) with the verb "*nuḥyiyannahu*" (فَلَنُحْيِيَنَّهُ) represents the strongest form of future promise, "We will surely give life."
4. It offers a dual reward: Beyond the good life in this world, there's also the promise of reward in the Hereafter based on the best of one's deeds.

But what exactly is this "ḥayātan ṭayyibah" (حَيَاةً طَيِّبَةً)? The Arabic word "ṭayyibah" carries connotations of goodness, wholesomeness, pleasantness, and purity. It describes something free from contamination or corruption, physically, morally, and spiritually.

The scholars have interpreted this "good life" as contentment, halal provision, satisfaction with what one has, and life with dignity. Together, these paint a picture of inner peace, sufficiency, and meaningful connection with the Divine, regardless of external circumstances.

The Garden Within

Perhaps no famous 13th century story exemplifies the reality of "ḥayātan ṭayyibah" more powerfully than Ibn Taymiyyah (ra), whose experience of imprisonment revealed the true nature of freedom and contentment.

Despite being unjustly imprisoned multiple times for his scholarly positions, Ibn Taymiyyah maintained an outlook so radiant that it confounded his persecutors. His student Ibn al-Qayyim reported that his teacher once told him:

مَا يَصْنَعُ أَعْدَائِي بِي ؟ أَنَا جَنَّتِي وَبُسْتَانِي فِي صَدْرِي؛ أَيْنَ رُحْتُ فَهِيَ مَعِي لَا تُفَارِقُنِي. أَنَا حَبْسِي خَلْوَةٌ، وَقَتْلِي شَهَادَةٌ، وَإِخْرَاجِي مِنْ بَلَدِي سِيَاحَةٌ

"What can my enemies do to me? My paradise and my garden are in my heart wherever I go. They are with me and never leave me. If I am imprisoned, it is seclusion for worship. If I am killed, it is martyrdom. If they expel me from my land, it is tourism."[57]

These remarkable words reveal a man who had discovered the secret of "ḥayātan ṭayyibah"—a life so deeply rooted in connection with Allah that external circumstances lost their power to determine his happiness. Behind prison walls, he experienced greater freedom than his jailers. Facing death, he saw the promise of martyrdom. Threatened with exile, he anticipated the joy of spiritual tourism.

This is not toxic positivity or denial of reality. Ibn Taymiyyah acknowledged his difficulties but reframed them through the lens of his relationship with Allah. His contentment wasn't despite his circumstances but transcended them entirely.

The Modern Search for Contentment

Despite unprecedented material abundance, contentment remains elusive for many. Ahmad, a successful executive, had achieved everything society promised would bring fulfillment—the corner office, luxury car, vacation home—yet felt persistent emptiness. The turning point came when he heard about the hadith: "He has succeeded who is guided to Islam, granted sufficient provision, and is content with it."[58]

"Success wasn't about accumulating more," Ahmad realized, "but recognizing sufficiency and cultivating contentment." He simplified his lifestyle and found greater fulfillment in serving others. His relationship with wealth fundamentally changed, it became a tool for good rather than a measure of worth.

Building the Foundation

How do we access this divine promise of a good life? The verse itself provides the formula: faith and righteous deeds. But within this framework, several key principles help us develop the mindset that enables ḥayātan ṭayyibah:

1. Know Who Allah Is

The foundation of a good life is an accurate understanding of who Allah ﷻ is in relation to our circumstances. As one scholar beautifully expressed:

> "Allah is bigger than your problems. Allah is greater than your opponents. Allah is greater than your anxieties. Allahu Akbar, Allahu Akbar, Allahu Akbar."

When we truly comprehend Allah's greatness, our problems are put into proper perspective. This isn't merely about repeating "Allahu Akbar" as a ritual on the tongue, but deeply internalizing its meaning until it transforms our perception of life's challenges.

2. Trust Allah's Wisdom Even in Pain

Recognizing Allah as Al-Hakeem (The All-Wise) enables us to trust that even painful experiences serve a greater purpose, whether we can discern it or not. This doesn't mean denying the pain but contextualizing it within divine wisdom.

The Prophet Ya'qub ﷺ provides a powerful example. When he lost his beloved son Yusuf, he experienced profound grief, weeping until he lost his eyesight. Yet he maintained unwavering trust in Allah, saying:

إِنَّمَا أَشْكُو بَثِّي وَحُزْنِي إِلَى اللَّهِ وَأَعْلَمُ مِنَ اللَّهِ مَا لَا تَعْلَمُونَ

"I only complain of my suffering and my grief to Allah, and I know from Allah that which you do not know." (12:86)

This balance, acknowledging genuine pain while maintaining trust in divine wisdom, characterizes the mature faith that produces "ḥayātan ṭayyibah."

A powerful contemporary example comes from Gaza, where a man who lost thirty relatives in a bombing was interviewed. Though his grief was palpable, he expressed a profound statement of faith: "We belong to Allah, and to Him we shall return. I am satisfied with Allah's decree, even in this immense trial."

Such testimonies remind us that sadness and contentment aren't mutually exclusive. One can experience deep sorrow while maintaining fundamental trust in Allah's wisdom, the essence of "ḥayātan ṭayyibah" even amid suffering.

3. Recognize Allah as Al-Wakeel (The Trustee)
Developing trust requires knowing Allah as Al-Wakeel, the ultimate and perfect trustee to whom we can entrust all our affairs.

The Prophet ﷺ exemplified this trust when he and Abu Bakr hid in the cave of Thawr during their migration to Madinah. With pursuers just outside, Abu Bakr whispered his concern: "If any of them looks down at his feet, he will see us!" The Prophet ﷺ responded with perfect tawakkul (trust): "What do you think of two people whose third is Allah?"[59]

This level of trust isn't achieved overnight but grows through consistent remembrance of Allah's attributes and reflection on His involvement in our lives. Each time we recognize Allah's subtle intervention or protection, our trust muscle strengthens.

The Role of Remembrance

At the heart of "ḥayātan ṭayyibah" lies a profound connection with Allah through consistent remembrance. Allah explicitly links tranquility of heart with dhikr:

الَّذِينَ آمَنُوا وَتَطْمَئِنُّ قُلُوبُهُم بِذِكْرِ اللَّهِ ۗ أَلَا بِذِكْرِ اللَّهِ تَطْمَئِنُّ الْقُلُوبُ

"Those who believe and whose hearts find comfort in the remembrance of Allah. Surely in the remembrance of Allah do hearts find comfort." (13:28)

This verse reveals that the tranquility we seek isn't found in external circumstances but in reconnecting with our Creator through conscious remembrance.

Faris, an ER nurse, discovered this amid chaos: "I practice dhikr while working, repeating 'SubḥānAllāh' between patients. This creates an inner sanctuary of calm even when everything is frantic."

Even brief moments of connection, thanking Allah for a meal, and seeking guidance before decisions, maintain the spiritual current that energizes "ḥayātan ṭayyibah."

Contentment: The Heart of a Good Life

The Arabic word "qanā'ah" (قناعة), contentment with what one has, emerges as perhaps the most essential quality of "ḥayātan ṭayyibah." The Prophet ﷺ emphasized its value when he said: "Richness is not having many possessions, but richness is the richness of the soul (contentment)."[60]

This profound statement redefines wealth entirely, locating it in an internal state rather than external accumulation. The truly wealthy person, by this definition, is the one whose heart is satisfied regardless of material circumstances.

Unlike material resources that diminish with use, contentment represents an inexhaustible treasury that remains accessible regardless of external conditions.

How do we cultivate this contentment? Several practices help nurture this quality:

1. Practicing gratitude for what we have rather than focusing on what we lack
2. Comparing downward by considering those with fewer blessings rather than those with more
3. Recognizing sufficiency by distinguishing between needs and wants
4. Detaching from outcomes while maintaining effort and trust in Allah

Nurturing contentment doesn't mean abandoning ambition or accepting injustice, rather, it means finding peace in our current circumstances while working toward improvement with detachment from specific outcomes.

Practical Steps Toward Ḥayātan Ṭayyibah

While the good life is ultimately a divine gift, we can cultivate the conditions that invite this blessing through practical steps:

1. Deepen your knowledge of Allah's names and attributes, focusing particularly on those that strengthen trust and contentment (Al-Wakeel, Al-Razzaq, Al-Kareem, Al-Hakeem)
2. Establish regular dhikr practices that maintain your connection with Allah throughout the day, not just during formal worship

3. Train yourself to see the wisdom behind difficulties by actively looking for potential benefits or lessons in every challenging situation
4. Simplify your material life by periodically evaluating your possessions and removing what doesn't contribute to your wellbeing or purpose
5. Practice gratitude deliberately by acknowledging specific blessings daily, especially those you might take for granted
6. Serve others with your unique gifts, recognizing that meaningful contribution is a core component of the good life
7. Cultivate quality relationships based on mutual support in righteousness rather than worldly interests
8. Align your work with your values so that your daily activities contribute to rather than detract from your spiritual wellbeing
9. Create boundaries around technology and media to protect your heart from comparison, discontent, and distraction
10. Remember death regularly as a perspective-restoring practice that clarifies priorities and diminishes attachment to temporary matters

These practices don't guarantee immediate transformation, but with consistency, they create the internal conditions where "ḥayātan ṭayyibah" can flourish.

The Promise That Transforms Our Understanding of Success

Allah's promise of a good life invites us to reconsider what constitutes success. The truly good life emerges not from favorable circumstances but from the internal condition of the heart. It's characterized not by the absence of challenges but by meaningful engagement with life grounded in faith and righteous action.

This liberates us from exhausting pursuit of external markers of success. Instead, it directs us toward cultivating internal resources—contentment, trust, gratitude, and connection with Allah—that remain accessible regardless of our situation.

Ibn Taymiyyah's words from prison weren't poetic exaggeration but lived reality: "My paradise and my garden are in my heart." This is available to every believer who meets Allah's conditions: faith and righteous deeds.

Regardless of where you find yourself today, in abundance or scarcity, health or illness, the path remains the same. Cultivate your relationship with Allah, align your actions with guidance, and nurture contentment with Allah's decree.

Discussion Questions

1. The chapter contrasts material wealth with inner richness. Can you recall a time when having "more" actually decreased your peace or contentment? What lesson did you learn from this experience?
2. Ibn Taymiyyah found freedom within imprisonment through his spiritual perspective. What current limitations or constraints in your life could be reframed as opportunities for spiritual growth?
3. The Prophet ﷺ said that the successful person is "guided to Islam, granted sufficient provision, and content with it." What constitutes "sufficient provision" in your life, and how might embracing the concept of "enough" (rather than "more") transform your sense of contentment?

"O Allah, rectify my religion which is the safeguard of my affairs, rectify my worldly life in which is my livelihood, and rectify my Hereafter to which is my return."

14

The Promise of Divine Forgiveness

Dhaka, Bangladesh

The evening prayer had just concluded when Imam Jameel noticed a young man lingering in the back of the masjid. While others filed out, exchanging warm greetings and making plans, this young man remained seated, his shoulders hunched, his gaze fixed on the prayer rug before him. There was a heaviness about him that spoke of a burden carried far too long.

As the hall emptied, Imam Jameel approached him gently. "As-salamu alaykum, my brother. Is there something I can help you with?"

The young man looked up, his eyes reflecting a storm of emotions—shame, fear, and a glimmer of desperate hope. "I don't know if anyone can help me," he said, his voice barely above a whisper. "I've made terrible mistakes."

"Would you like to talk about it?" the imam offered, sitting beside him.

After a moment's hesitation, the young man began to speak. He described how he had been raised in a practicing Muslim family but had drifted during his college years. "I fell in with the wrong crowd," he explained. "Started drinking, experimented with drugs, engaged in relationships I shouldn't have... I even stopped praying entirely for almost two years."

His voice caught. "The worst part is, I knew better. My parents taught me right from wrong. But I ignored everything for the sake of fitting in, for temporary pleasures that left me feeling hollow. I feel severe guilt and pain and disgust with myself."

Now, having graduated and started working, Ali had begun to feel the full weight of his choices. "Recently, I've been having nightmares about standing before Allah on the Day of Judgment with nothing to offer but these sins. I've started praying again, but..." His eyes welled with tears. "Will Allah ever forgive me? After all I've done, deliberately turning away from what I knew was right—is there any hope for someone like me?"

Imam Hassan's eyes softened with compassion. He reached for the Qur'an copy on the shelf beside them, opened it to Surat Az-Zumar, and gently placed it in Ali's hands. "Can you read this verse?" he asked, pointing to the 53rd ayah.

Ali began to read, his voice trembling:

قُلْ يَا عِبَادِيَ الَّذِينَ أَسْرَفُوا عَلَىٰ أَنفُسِهِمْ لَا تَقْنَطُوا مِن رَّحْمَةِ اللَّهِ ۚ إِنَّ اللَّهَ يَغْفِرُ الذُّنُوبَ جَمِيعًا ۚ إِنَّهُ هُوَ الْغَفُورُ الرَّحِيمُ

"Say, 'O My servants who have transgressed against themselves, do not despair of the mercy of Allah. Indeed, Allah forgives all sins. Indeed, it is He who is the Forgiving, the Merciful.'" (39:53)

As he finished reading, Ali looked up with the first stirrings of hope. "All sins?" he said. "Even mine?"

"Yes, brother," Imam Jameel replied gently. "Even yours. This verse wasn't revealed for the angels or for those who never sin. It was revealed precisely for people like you and me—those who recognize their mistakes and seek to sincerely return to their Lord. Allah's mercy is greater than you can imagine, and His promise of forgiveness to the sincere repentant is one of the most beautiful guarantees in our faith."

Ali asked, "But how do I know if my repentance is accepted? How can I be sure?"

"That," said Imam Jameel with a smile, "is what I'd like to share with you today."

The Divine Promise of Forgiveness

Throughout the Qur'an, Allah's promise to forgive the sincere repentant stands as one of the most repeated and emphasized guarantees. This isn't a minor theme or a footnote—it's a central aspect of Allah's relationship with His creation, mentioned dozens of times in various forms.

Consider the comprehensive nature of this promise in Surat Al-Nisa:

وَمَن يَعْمَلْ سُوءًا أَوْ يَظْلِمْ نَفْسَهُ ثُمَّ يَسْتَغْفِرِ اللَّهَ يَجِدِ اللَّهَ غَفُورًا رَّحِيمًا

"And whoever does wrong or wrongs himself but then seeks forgiveness of Allah will find Allah Forgiving and Merciful." (4:110)

The language here is both simple and profound. There are no complicated conditions, no bureaucratic processes, no intermediaries required, just a direct relationship between the servant who seeks forgiveness and the Lord who is characterized by forgiveness and mercy.

Notice the certainty in the phrase "will find" (يَجِدِ). This isn't presented as a possibility or a probability but as an absolute guarantee—the repentant servant will find Allah Forgiving and Merciful.

Beyond Forgiveness: The Transformation of Sins

While forgiveness itself would be an immense blessing, Allah's generosity extends even further. In one of the most hope-inspiring verses of the Qur'an, Allah promises not just to erase sins but to transform them into good deeds:

إِلَّا مَن تَابَ وَآمَنَ وَعَمِلَ عَمَلًا صَالِحًا فَأُولَٰئِكَ يُبَدِّلُ اللَّهُ سَيِّئَاتِهِمْ حَسَنَاتٍ ۗ
وَكَانَ اللَّهُ غَفُورًا رَّحِيمًا

"Except for those who repent, believe, and do righteous deeds. For them, Allah will replace their evil deeds with good deeds. And Allah is ever Forgiving and Merciful." (25:70)

Imagine the magnitude of this promise. The very actions that once weighed heavy on your record, that caused you shame and regret, can be transformed into sources of reward. This verse appears in Surat Al-Furqan immediately after the mention of major sins including shirk (associating partners with Allah), murder, and adultery. Even these grave transgressions can be transformed through sincere repentance.

This divine accounting defies human logic. In worldly terms, the best we typically hope for after a serious mistake is that it might be forgotten or overlooked. But Allah offers something far greater: the transformation of our worst moments into our spiritual assets.

The Man Who Killed 100

The Prophet ﷺ told of a man who killed ninety-nine people. Seeking forgiveness, he asked a monk if there was hope. The monk incorrectly said no, so the man killed him too, making it one hundred.

A knowledgeable scholar then assured him: "Yes, go to such-and-such land where people worship Allah and do not return to your land of evil."

The man died on his journey. When angels disputed over his soul, Allah commanded them to measure which land he was closer to. He was closer to righteousness by a handspan, so the angels of mercy took him.[61]

Even one hundred murders couldn't place him beyond Allah's mercy when his repentance was sincere and he began the physical act of repentance. This has no impact on the rights that were taken from the victims, as Allah will reward them with so much more.

The Barriers to Seeking Forgiveness

If Allah's forgiveness is so readily available, what prevents us from seeking it? Several internal barriers often hold people back:

1. Despair of Allah's Mercy

Some believe their sins are too great or numerous to be forgiven. This despair itself becomes a serious spiritual problem, as it implies a limitation on Allah's mercy.

Allah directly addresses this mindset in the verse that Imam Jameel showed to Ali.

The phrase "all sins" (الذُّنُوبَ جَمِيعًا) leaves no room for exception. There is no category of sin that lies beyond Allah's capacity to forgive, provided one turns to Him in sincere repentance while their hearts yet beat (and before the sun rises from the West for the end times to begin).

2. Procrastination

Others acknowledge Allah's forgiveness but delay seeking it, assuming there will always be time later. This dangerous assumption, intertwined with pride, ignores the uncertainty of life and the potential hardening of the heart through persistent sin.

Allah warns against this mentality:

إِنَّمَا التَّوْبَةُ عَلَى اللَّهِ لِلَّذِينَ يَعْمَلُونَ السُّوءَ بِجَهَالَةٍ ثُمَّ يَتُوبُونَ مِن قَرِيبٍ فَأُولَٰئِكَ يَتُوبُ اللَّهُ عَلَيْهِمْ ۗ
وَكَانَ اللَّهُ عَلِيمًا حَكِيمًا

"Repentance accepted by Allah is only for those who do wrong in ignorance and then repent soon after. It is those to whom Allah will turn in forgiveness, and Allah is ever Knowing and Wise." (4:17)

While this verse emphasizes the importance of prompt repentance, other verses and hadith make clear that the door of repentance remains open until the moment of death or until the sun rises from the west (a sign of the Day of Judgment). Nevertheless, the emphasis on not delaying is a crucial reminder.

3. Pride and Shame

Sometimes pride prevents us from acknowledging our mistakes, or shame keeps us from facing our actions honestly. Both can block the path to sincere repentance. Allah reminds us that He knows our deeds, whether we acknowledge them or not:

وَهُوَ الَّذِي يَقْبَلُ التَّوْبَةَ عَنْ عِبَادِهِ وَيَعْفُو عَنِ السَّيِّئَاتِ وَيَعْلَمُ مَا تَفْعَلُونَ

"And it is He who accepts repentance from His servants and pardons misdeeds, and He knows what you do." (42:25)

Since Allah already knows our sins, pride and shame serve no purpose except to keep us distant from His mercy. We are required to act upon our knowledge and wanting His forgiveness.

Modern Journeys of Return

Ahmed, a former drug dealer, changed when a customer nearly died from an overdose. "I had blood on my hands," he realized.

At a Friday sermon about divine forgiveness, he heard:

وَالَّذِينَ عَمِلُوا السَّيِّئَاتِ ثُمَّ تَابُوا مِن بَعْدِهَا وَآمَنُوا إِنَّ رَبَّكَ مِن بَعْدِهَا لَغَفُورٌ رَّحِيمٌ

'But those who committed evil deeds and afterward repented and believed—indeed your Lord, thereafter, is surely Forgiving and Merciful.' (7:153)

"Something broke open in me," Ahmed recalled. He eventually left his former life, found legitimate work, and now works with at-risk youth. "My past gives me credibility with these kids. What was once my greatest shame has become an effective tool for good."

The Requirements of Sincere Repentance

While Allah's forgiveness is vast, repentance must meet certain conditions to be considered sincere. Scholars have traditionally outlined three essential components (or four, when rights of others are involved):

1. Immediate Cessation of the Sin
The first step is to stop the sinful behavior immediately. Claiming to repent while continuing the very action one is supposedly repenting is prideful.

2. Genuine Remorse for the Action
True repentance involves regret, not merely for the consequences of the sin but for having disobeyed Allah. This remorse is the spiritual pain that leads to healing, as the Prophet ﷺ said: "The one who repents from sin is like one who has no sin."[62]

3. Firm Resolve Never to Return to the Sin
Sincere repentance includes a determined intention not to repeat the sin. While humans may slip again due to weakness (requiring renewed repentance), approaching repentance with an intention to return to the sin invalidates it.

4. Rectifying the Rights of Others (When Applicable)
If the sin involved harming others or taking their rights, complete repentance requires making amends where possible, returning stolen property, compensating for damages, or seeking forgiveness from those wronged.

Allah ﷻ Wants to Forgive

One of the most beautiful aspects of Islamic teaching on repentance is the portrayal of Allah as not merely willing to forgive but actually eager to do so. The Prophet ﷺ conveyed this in a profound hadith qudsi:

> "Allah the Exalted says: 'I am as My servant thinks of Me, and I am with him when he remembers Me. If he remembers Me within himself, I remember him within Myself; if he remembers Me in a gathering, I remember him in a better gathering. If he draws near to Me by a handspan, I draw near to him by an arm's length; if he draws near to Me by an arm's length, I draw near to him by a fathom; and if he comes to Me walking, I come to him running.'"[63]

This hadith reveals Allah's eagerness to respond to even the smallest movement of His servant toward Him. Far from being reluctant to forgive, Allah hastens toward the repentant with greater speed than they approach Him.

Another hadith further illustrates this divine eagerness for reconciliation: "Allah is more delighted with the repentance of His servant than one of you would be about finding his camel which had strayed away from him in the desert."[64]

The imagery is striking; Allah's joy at our repentance exceeds the desperate relief of a desert traveler who, facing certain death without transportation or water, suddenly recovers the lost camel that represents survival itself.

Allah's Many Names of Forgiveness

The importance of forgiveness in Allah's relationship with humanity is underscored by the multiple divine names that relate to this attribute. Each name highlights a different aspect of His all-encompassing mercy:

1. Al-Ghafoor (الْغَفُورُ) - The Most Forgiving, repeatedly forgiving the same mistakes
2. Al-Ghaffar (الْغَفَّارُ) - The Perpetual Forgiver, continuously forgiving all sins
3. Al-'Afuw (الْعَفُوُّ) - The Pardoner, who effaces sins completely
4. At-Tawwāb (التَّوَّابُ) - The Acceptor of Repentance, who facilitates and welcomes return

This rich vocabulary of forgiveness in Allah's self-description reveals how central this attribute is to His relationship with us. As He states:

وَإِنِّي لَغَفَّارٌ لِّمَن تَابَ وَآمَنَ وَعَمِلَ صَالِحًا ثُمَّ اهْتَدَىٰ

"But indeed, I am the Perpetual Forgiver of whoever repents and believes and does righteousness and then continues in guidance." (20:82)

The Continuous Journey of Return

A final crucial aspect of Islamic teaching on repentance is its ongoing nature. Rather than a one-time event, tawbah (repentance) represents a continuous attitude of returning to Allah throughout life.

The Prophet ﷺ embodied this principle, saying: "O people, repent to Allah, for I repent to Allah one hundred times a day."[65] If the best of creation, a man whose past and future sins were already forgiven, maintained this practice of constant return to Allah, how much more should we cultivate this habit?

This continuous repentance isn't about repeatedly falling into major sins but about maintaining spiritual sensitivity, acknowledging even subtle lapses, and constantly refreshing our commitment to Allah.

The Promise that Renews Hope

Let us return to Ali. As Imam Jameel shared these truths, the young man's burden visibly lifted. "Allah has no need for our worship," the imam explained. "Nothing we do benefits or harms Him. Yet He continuously invites us back, no matter how many times we turn away. The very fact that your heart feels remorse is already a sign of His mercy reaching out to you."

Each of us carries burdens of regret. To all, Allah extends His timeless promise:

إِلَّا مَن تَابَ وَآمَنَ وَعَمِلَ عَمَلًا صَالِحًا فَأُولَٰئِكَ يُبَدِّلُ اللَّهُ سَيِّئَاتِهِمْ حَسَنَاتٍ

"For them, Allah will replace their evil deeds with good deeds. And Allah is ever Forgiving and Merciful." (25:70)

This isn't merely cancellation of debt but merciful transformation, as the acts that once distanced us from Allah become the means by which we draw closer to Him.

Whatever sins burden your heart today, Allah's door remains open. The Prophet ﷺ assured us: "Allah extends His hand during the night so that those who committed sins during the day may repent, and He extends His hand during the day so that those who committed sins during the night may repent."[66]

May we recognize this profound gift, a promise that transforms our darkest moments into opportunities for light, our deepest regrets into catalysts for growth, and our sinful past into a future bright with the pleasure of our Lord.

Discussion Questions

1. The chapter mentions that our sins can become "stepping stones" toward spiritual growth. Reflect on a mistake or sin in your past that ultimately led to positive growth in your faith or character. How did this experience change your understanding of Allah's wisdom and mercy?
2. We learned about the three essential components of sincere repentance: stopping the sin immediately, feeling genuine remorse, and resolving never to return to it (plus making amends when others' rights are involved). Which of these aspects do you find most challenging in your own journey of repentance, and why?
3. The hadith describes Allah as being "more delighted with the repentance of His servant than one of you would be about finding his camel which had strayed away from him in the desert." How might truly internalizing this image of Allah's eagerness to forgive change your approach to seeking forgiveness after making mistakes?

"O Allah, You are Most Forgiving and Generous, You love forgiveness, so forgive me."

15

The Promise of Reciprocal Forgiveness

Cape Town, South Africa

The conference room fell silent as Ahmed finished his presentation. The investment committee exchanged glances, some impressed, others skeptical. For Ahmed, this pitch represented months of preparation and years of entrepreneurial vision. His clean energy startup needed this funding to survive.

"Thank you for your time," Ahmed concluded, gathering his materials as the committee members filed out to deliberate.

As he packed up, Ahmed noticed Haris, the committee's most vocal skeptic, lingering behind. Three years ago, Haris had been Ahmed's business partner in a previous venture. Their partnership had ended bitterly when Haris suddenly pulled out, taking a key client with him and nearly bankrupting Ahmed's fledgling company.

Ahmed had avoided Haris ever since, declining invitations to industry events where they might cross paths. The wound still felt fresh, not just the financial blow, but the betrayal by someone he had trusted. When he discovered Haris was on this investment committee, Ahmed had seriously considered withdrawing his application altogether.

"Your technology has improved considerably since your last prototype," Haris said, approaching cautiously.

Ahmed nodded stiffly, struggling to maintain professional composure. "We've addressed the efficiency issues."

An uncomfortable silence hung between them before Haris spoke again, his voice quieter now. "Listen, Ahmed. I know this is awkward. What happened between us… I've regretted it for years. I was going through a divorce, my father was ill, and

I made desperate decisions. I'm not justifying it, just trying to explain. I'm truly sorry for the harm I caused you."

Ahmed felt the familiar anger rising, the countless sleepless nights, the investors who had backed out, the employees he'd had to let go. "It's a bit late for apologies, isn't it?"

"Perhaps," Haris acknowledged. "But I needed to say it anyway. I'm not expecting any forgiveness or compassion as I was fully wrong. The guilt has kept me up on countless nights and I feel sincerely remorseful." He turned to leave, then paused. "Regardless of what happened between us, your current project deserves fair consideration. I'll be recusing myself from the committee's decision to ensure there's no conflict of interest."

As Haris reached the door, a verse from the Qur'an suddenly surfaced in Ahmed's mind, words he had recited countless times without fully contemplating their personal application:

وَلْيَعْفُوا وَلْيَصْفَحُوا ۗ أَلَا تُحِبُّونَ أَن يَغْفِرَ اللَّهُ لَكُمْ ۗ وَاللَّهُ غَفُورٌ رَّحِيمٌ

"Let them pardon and forgive. Do you not love that Allah should forgive you? And Allah is Forgiving and Merciful." (24:22)

The words struck him with new force. *Do you not love that Allah should forgive you?* Of course he did, he prayed for Allah's forgiveness daily. Yet here he was, clutching tightly to his resentment, unwilling to extend to Haris the very forgiveness he hoped to receive from his Lord.

"Haris," Ahmed called. "I appreciate your apology. It wasn't excusable, what you did. But... I forgive you."

The words felt strange as they left his lips, yet they carried an unexpected lightness with them. Ahmed was surprised to discover that he meant them.

The Divine Connection Between Giving and Receiving Forgiveness

Among Allah's most practical promises is the direct connection He establishes between our forgiveness of others and His forgiveness of us. This reciprocal relationship appears in various forms throughout the Qur'an and hadith, creating a powerful incentive for believers to cultivate forgiveness in their dealings with others. In Surat An-Nur, Allah poses a profound question:

وَلْيَعْفُوا وَلْيَصْفَحُوا ۗ أَلَا تُحِبُّونَ أَن يَغْفِرَ اللَّهُ لَكُمْ ۗ وَاللَّهُ غَفُورٌ رَّحِيمٌ

"Let them pardon and forgive. Do you not love that Allah should forgive you? And Allah is Forgiving and Merciful." (24:22)

This rhetorical question strikes at the heart of human inconsistency. We all desire Allah's forgiveness for our transgressions, yet we often withhold forgiveness from those who have wronged us. The verse highlights this contradiction and invites us to align our behavior toward others with what we seek from Allah.

The Prophet ﷺ made this connection even more explicit: "Show mercy to those on earth, and the One in the Heaven will show mercy to you."[67]

This principle extends beyond mere divine suggestion to become a determining factor in Allah's treatment of us. The Prophet ﷺ elaborated: "Whoever does not show mercy will not be shown mercy."[68] These teachings establish a clear spiritual law: our reception of divine mercy and forgiveness is directly connected to our extension of these qualities to others.

Beyond Transaction

While the promise of reciprocal forgiveness might initially appear transactional, forgive others so Allah will forgive you, Islamic teachings encourage a deeper understanding that transforms forgiveness from a spiritual bargaining chip into a genuine expression of character.

Allah describes the people of taqwā (God-consciousness) as:

الَّذِينَ يُنفِقُونَ فِي السَّرَّاءِ وَالضَّرَّاءِ وَالْكَاظِمِينَ الْغَيْظَ وَالْعَافِينَ عَنِ النَّاسِ ۗ
وَاللَّهُ يُحِبُّ الْمُحْسِنِينَ

"Those who spend [in the cause of Allah] during ease and hardship and who restrain anger and who pardon the people - and Allah loves the doers of good." (3:134)

Here, pardoning people is presented not as a transaction to secure divine favor but as an attribute of the spiritually excellent, whom "Allah loves." The motivation shifts from securing personal benefit to embodying divine attributes.

Farah, a family counselor, observed this transformation in her own journey: "Initially, I forgave difficult family members because I wanted Allah's forgiveness for myself. But over time, something changed. I began to forgive because I recognized that holding onto resentment damaged me more than them, and because forgiveness aligned me with the divine qualities I aspired to embody. It became less about what I could get and more about who I wanted to be."

When Forgiveness Seems Impossible

Some wrongs appear so severe that forgiveness seems beyond human capacity. Samira's brother was killed by a drunk driver. "I thought forgiveness would betray his memory," she recalled.

Her perspective shifted when she reflected on the Prophet ﷺ at Tā'if. After being brutally assaulted, he was offered divine assistance to destroy the city. Instead, he prayed: "O Allah, guide my people, for they do not know."[69]

Years later, Samira met the driver through a restorative justice program. "The forgiveness I offered freed us both, him from crushing guilt, and me from the prison of hatred I had built." It also ended up being the driver's catalyst into Islam.

Forgiveness Versus Justice

An important clarification in Islamic teachings is that forgiveness does not necessarily mean abandoning justice. The Qur'an acknowledges the legitimacy of proportional response to harm:

وَجَزَاءُ سَيِّئَةٍ سَيِّئَةٌ مِّثْلُهَا ۖ فَمَنْ عَفَا وَأَصْلَحَ فَأَجْرُهُ عَلَى اللَّهِ ۚ إِنَّهُ لَا يُحِبُّ الظَّالِمِينَ

"And the retribution for an evil act is an evil one like it, but whoever pardons and makes reconciliation - his reward is [due] from Allah. Indeed, He does not like wrongdoers." (42:40)

This verse presents both options, seeking proportional justice or choosing forgiveness, while indicating that forgiveness carries special divine reward. Furthermore, this entire chapter on forgiveness as a noble act does not imply taking lightly any ongoing, current abuse in one's life, or to be passive or a pacifist.

Imam Mujahid, who works extensively with both victims and perpetrators of crime, explains this balance: "Islamic justice principles acknowledge the victim's right to seek appropriate redress. Forgiveness is presented as a virtuous choice, not an obligation that enables continued oppression. Sometimes justice must be served first to create the conditions where genuine forgiveness becomes possible."

This nuanced approach prevents both extremes: neither allowing forgiveness to become a tool that enables continued harm, nor permitting justice to devolve into vindictiveness.

The Double Liberation of Forgiveness

Modern psychology has caught up with what Islamic teachings have long asserted—forgiveness benefits the forgiver as much as, if not more than, the forgiven. Research shows that practicing forgiveness correlates with reduced depression, anxiety, and stress, along with improved heart health and immune function. The divine reward for anger suppression (a component of forgiveness) highlights both immediate psychological benefits and eternal rewards.

As one psychologist observed, "Holding resentment chains you to both the person who harmed you and the painful event. Forgiveness cuts those chains."

Practical Steps Toward Forgiveness

For those struggling with forgiveness, Islamic tradition offers practical approaches:

1. Remember Your Own Need for Forgiveness
The Prophet ﷺ taught a prayer that highlights our shared need for divine mercy:

اللَّهُمَّ إِنَّكَ عَفُوٌّ تُحِبُّ الْعَفْوَ فَاعْفُ عَنِّي

"O Allah, You are Pardoning and love pardon, so pardon me."[70]

Regularly acknowledging our own mistakes and need for forgiveness creates the psychological foundation for extending forgiveness to others.

2. Separate the Person from the Action
Islamic ethics distinguishes between condemning harmful actions and condemning the person who committed them. The Qur'an consistently speaks of "those who believe and do righteous deeds" rather than creating fixed identities based on behavior.

Layla applied this principle when dealing with a colleague who had taken credit for her work. "I reminded myself to hate the action but not the person. When I separated these, I could see her insecurity and the pressure she was under. It didn't justify what she did, but it helped me see her humanity rather than reducing her to a typical 'thief' in my mind." She still pursued the credit she deserved, but with less of a grudge in her own heart.

3. Consider the Example of Prophetic Forgiveness
The Prophet Muhammad's ﷺ life provides remarkable examples of forgiveness, culminating in his treatment of the people of Makkah who had persecuted him and his followers for years. Upon conquering the city, he asked them, "What do you think I will do with you?" They expected revenge based on the standards of their time, but instead, he declared:

لَا تَثْرِيبَ عَلَيْكُمُ الْيَوْمَ يَغْفِرُ اللَّهُ لَكُمْ وَهُوَ أَرْحَمُ الرَّاحِمِينَ

"There is no blame upon you today. May Allah forgive you, and He is the most merciful of the merciful." (12:92)

Reflecting on this magnanimity toward those who had caused him immense suffering provides perspective on our comparatively minor grievances.

4. Start with Small Forgiveness
For those facing severe betrayal or harm, beginning with forgiving smaller offenses can build the "forgiveness muscle" needed for more significant challenges.

The Promise That Liberates

The promise connecting our forgiveness of others with Allah's forgiveness operates on multiple levels, it's simultaneously a spiritual law, psychological principle, and path to social harmony.

When we withhold forgiveness, believing we're punishing the other person, we often imprison ourselves while constricting Allah's mercy toward us. By choosing to forgive, we unlock both divine mercy and our own emotional freedom.

This doesn't mean forgetting harm or reconciling with those who remain dangerous. Rather, it means releasing the burning coal of resentment that damages us more than anyone else.

Discussion Questions

1. Think about a situation where you're struggling to forgive someone. How might your desire for Allah's forgiveness help shift your perspective toward this person?
2. The chapter mentioned how forgiveness benefits the forgiver psychologically and spiritually. Have you experienced the "double liberation" of forgiveness in your own life? How did forgiving someone change your internal state?
3. Islamic tradition distinguishes between forgiveness and enabling continued harm. In what situations might establishing boundaries or seeking justice be necessary alongside forgiveness? How can we maintain a forgiving heart while also protecting ourselves or others from ongoing harm?

"O Allah, forgive my sins, my errors, my ignorance, and forgive what I have done before and after, what I have concealed and what I have done openly."

16

The Promise of Divine Remembrance

New York City, New York

The subway platform was packed with evening commuters, the air thick with exhaust and impatience. Sami stood pressed against the wall, his prayer beads moving steadily through his fingers despite the chaos around him. At forty-five, he had been making this commute for nearly two decades, but today felt different. The layoff notice in his briefcase seemed to weigh heavier with each passing minute.

A young man beside him noticed his quiet recitation and the peace on his face amid the surrounding stress. “Excuse me,” he said gently, “I don’t mean to intrude, but there’s something... calming about your presence. I’ve been having panic attacks on this platform for weeks, but hearing you, I feel different.”

Sami looked up, recognizing the exhaustion in his eyes, the same look he’d seen in his own mirror many mornings. “I understand that feeling,” he replied. “Three hours ago, I received news that turned my world upside down. But I’ve learned something that has carried me through every storm in my life.”

He paused as the approaching train’s rumble filled the tunnel. “No matter where I am, even here, in this crowded, stressful place, I am never alone. When I remember God, He remembers me.”

The Reciprocal Promise

Among Allah’s many guarantees to humanity, the promise of divine remembrance stands as one of the most immediate and accessible. Unlike promises that will be fulfilled in the future or after certain conditions are met, this promise offers an instantaneous divine response to human action:

فَاذْكُرُونِي أَذْكُرْكُمْ

“So remember Me; I will remember you.” (2:152)

In just a few Arabic words, Allah establishes a direct reciprocal relationship between human remembrance and divine attention. The Creator of the universe, who needs nothing and depends on nothing, promises to turn His specific attention toward any servant who remembers Him.

To appreciate the magnitude of this promise, we must understand what it means for Allah to "remember" His servant. Unlike human remembrance, which might be fleeting or forgetful, divine remembrance involves perfect attention, mercy, and assistance. When Allah remembers His servant, this manifests as guidance, protection, provision, and drawing that servant closer to divine presence.

The Effects of Dhikr

Remembrance of Allah (dhikr) encompasses a spectrum of practices, from formal liturgical recitations to the silent remembrance of the heart. Each form carries the same divine promise of reciprocal attention, creating both external and internal transformations.

A Muslim neuropsychologist who studies the effects of Islamic spiritual practices described the measurable impact of consistent dhikr: "From a scientific perspective, regular dhikr practice appears to activate the parasympathetic nervous system—our body's 'rest and digest' mode—counteracting the stress response. MRI studies show increased activity in brain regions associated with focus, emotional regulation, and empathy among those who maintain consistent remembrance practices."

While these physiological effects are significant, the internal spiritual transformation runs deeper. As Allah states:

أَلَا بِذِكْرِ اللَّهِ تَطْمَئِنُّ الْقُلُوبُ

"Truly, in the remembrance of Allah do hearts find rest." (13:28)

This "rest" (طمأنينة - ṭuma'neenah) isn't merely the absence of anxiety but the presence of a positive tranquility that anchors the heart despite external turbulence.

Zainab, a social worker who counsels refugees who have experienced severe trauma, observed this phenomenon repeatedly: "I've worked with people who lost everything, homes, family members, their entire way of life. Among those who recover most effectively are those who maintain a practice of remembering Allah consistently. This remembrance doesn't erase their grief or traumatic memories, but it provides a sacred space of safety within the ongoing difficulty."

Remembrance Amidst Distraction

Our devices create "continuous partial attention"—perpetually fragmented awareness. This makes intentional remembrance critical as a counter-practice.

One approach is "dhikr anchoring"—attaching remembrances to routine activities: saying 'Bismillah' when washing hands, 'Alhamdulillah' when checking phones, 'Subhan Allah' between tasks. These micro-practices create windows for divine connection throughout the day, following the Prophetic model of maintaining remembrance in all states.

Remembrance in Adversity

After a house fire destroyed everything, Maria found herself in a shelter with three children, her husband hospitalized with severe burns. In that darkest moment, she began reciting:

حَسْبِيَ اللَّهُ لَا إِلَٰهَ إِلَّا هُوَ ۖ عَلَيْهِ تَوَكَّلْتُ ۖ وَهُوَ رَبُّ الْعَرْشِ الْعَظِيمِ

"Sufficient for me is Allah; there is no deity except Him. On Him I have relied, and He is the Lord of the Great Throne." (9:129)

"By dawn, nothing external had changed," she explained. "But I had changed. I had certainty that Allah was with us, remembering us as we remembered Him. This didn't prevent hardship but provided an unshakeable foundation."

Four Dimensions of Divine Remembrance

Scholars have identified multiple dimensions to Allah's remembrance of those who remember Him:

1. Remembrance with Mercy and Forgiveness
When we remember Allah, He remembers us with mercy and forgiveness. The Prophet ﷺ conveyed this in a hadith qudsi: "Allah the Exalted says: 'I am as My servant thinks of Me, and I am with him when he remembers Me.'"[71]

This divine companionship during remembrance represents a special mercy that surrounds the servant who engages in dhikr.

2. Remembrance with Protection
Allah's remembrance of His servant includes protection from harm. The Prophet ﷺ taught a powerful morning and evening remembrance:

بِسْمِ اللَّهِ الَّذِي لَا يَضُرُّ مَعَ اسْمِهِ شَيْءٌ فِي الْأَرْضِ وَلَا فِي السَّمَاءِ وَهُوَ السَّمِيعُ الْعَلِيمُ

"In the name of Allah, with Whose name nothing can cause harm on earth or in the heaven, and He is the All-Hearing, the All-Knowing."[72]

The Prophet ﷺ said that whoever recites this three times in the morning and evening, nothing will harm them. This protection represents a manifestation of Allah's remembrance of the servant who remembers Him.

3. Remembrance with Guidance
When Allah remembers His servant, He provides guidance in decisions and direction in life. Allah states:

وَالَّذِينَ جَاهَدُوا فِينَا لَنَهْدِيَنَّهُمْ سُبُلَنَا

"And those who strive for Us - We will surely guide them to Our ways." (29:69)

This guidance often manifests as intuitive clarity about which path to take at critical junctures.

4. Remembrance with Elevation
Perhaps the most profound dimension of Allah's remembrance is the elevation of the servant's rank and status with Him. The Prophet ﷺ reported that Allah says: "Whoever remembers Me within himself, I remember him within Myself. And whoever remembers Me in a gathering, I remember him in a gathering better than it."[73] This "better gathering" refers to the assembly of angels, a spiritual elevation that transcends any worldly status or recognition.

Practices of Remembrance

While Islamic tradition offers numerous specific formulas for dhikr, the effectiveness of remembrance depends less on quantity or specific wording than on the quality of presence and sincerity behind it.

The Prophet ﷺ said: "The example of the one who remembers his Lord and the one who does not remember his Lord is like that of the living and the dead."[74] This stark comparison emphasizes that remembrance is not a supplementary spiritual practice but essential to the soul's vital functioning.

For those seeking to develop or deepen their practice of remembrance, consider these approaches:

1. Morning and Evening Adhkār
The Prophet ﷺ established specific remembrances for morning and evening, creating spiritual bookends to the day. These include glorification of Allah (tasbīḥ), seeking forgiveness (istighfār), and supplications for protection.

Start with just one or two of these prophetic remembrances, focusing on understanding their meaning and reciting them with presence rather than rushing through a lengthy list mechanically.

2. Remembrance After Obligatory Prayers

The moments following each obligatory prayer offer a special opportunity for remembrance. The Prophet ﷺ regularly recited:

أَسْتَغْفِرُ اللَّهَ (three times)

اللَّهُمَّ أَنْتَ السَّلَامُ، وَمِنْكَ السَّلَامُ، تَبَارَكْتَ يَا ذَا الْجَلَالِ وَالْإِكْرَامِ

"I seek forgiveness from Allah" (three times) "O Allah, You are Peace, and from You comes peace. Blessed are You, O Owner of majesty and honor." (Muslim)

Followed by 33 repetitions each of "Subhan Allah" (Glory be to Allah), "Alhamdulillah" (All praise is due to Allah), and "Allahu Akbar" (Allah is Greatest), and completing the hundred with "*La ilaha illAllah wahdahu la shareeka lah, lahul mulk wa lahul hamd, wa huwa 'ala kulli shay'in qadeer*" (There is no deity except Allah alone, with no partner. To Him belongs the dominion and all praise, and He is over all things competent).

3. Heart-Present Remembrance Throughout the Day

Beyond formal practices, cultivate an awareness that remembers Allah during ordinary activities. The early Muslims would engage in dhikr while walking in the market, working with their hands, or engaging in household tasks.

Asma, a widowed mother of four who works full-time, described how she integrated this practice: "I transformed routine activities into remembrance opportunities. While chopping vegetables, I recite 'Alhamdulillah' with each cut. Folding laundry becomes 'Subhan Allah' with each item. Stuck in traffic, I remember Allah instead of growing frustrated. These micro-moments of remembrance throughout my day have gradually altered my perception of daily life from mundane to meaningful."

4. Remembrance in Nature

Natural settings often facilitate deeper remembrance by displaying Allah's creative power and beauty. The Qur'an repeatedly directs our attention to natural phenomena as signs (āyāt) pointing to their Creator.

Spending time in natural environments while consciously engaging in dhikr, whether through traditional formulas or simply contemplating Allah's names and attributes as manifested in creation, can powerfully unite external and internal forms of remembrance.

Communal Remembrance

While personal remembrance carries the divine promise of reciprocal attention, remembrance in community creates a special atmosphere that the Prophet Muhammad ﷺ described vividly: "No people gather in one of the houses of Allah, reciting the Book of Allah and studying it together, except that tranquility descends upon them, mercy covers them, the angels surround them, and Allah mentions them to those who are with Him."[75]

This hadith describes a remarkable scene, human remembrance of Allah through studying His Book leads to His remembering them among the heavenly host.

Many who participate in group study (e.g., community lectures) describe a palpable energy and fulfilling experience that sometimes exceeds individual practice. Psychologically, this makes sense, as communal worship creates social reinforcement and shared focus. Spiritually, it reflects the divine promise of special recognition for those who remember Allah collectively.

The Cost of Forgetting

The promise of divine remembrance has a sobering corollary: those who forget Allah risk being spiritually forgotten by Him. Allah warns us in the Qur'an:

وَلَا تَكُونُوا كَالَّذِينَ نَسُوا اللَّهَ فَأَنسَاهُمْ أَنفُسَهُمْ ۚ أُولَٰئِكَ هُمُ الْفَاسِقُونَ

"And be not like those who forgot Allah, so He made them forget themselves. Those are the defiantly disobedient." (59:19)

This spiritual forgetfulness doesn't mean Allah ceases to know the person, as His knowledge encompasses all things. Rather, it refers to being deprived of the special attention, guidance, and protection that come with divine remembrance.

This spiritual condition manifests as a profound disorientation—forgetting not just Allah but one's own true nature and purpose. When we forget the divine, we lose perspective on our own identity as Allah's servants and vicegerents on earth.

Modern psychology offers a parallel concept in "identity foreclosure"—when individuals commit to identities without proper exploration, often adopting values and goals that don't reflect their authentic selves. From an Islamic perspective, this represents a profound consequence of forgetting Allah—we lose access to our divinely ordained purpose and potential.

The Promise That Transforms Every Moment

The divine promise of reciprocal remembrance transforms how we experience every moment. This isn't a distant promise but an immediate reality available now, regardless of circumstances.

Whether in a hospital waiting room, celebrating success, or facing loss, the same guarantee applies: when you remember Allah, He remembers you.

One scholar described it beautifully: "Remembrance is to the heart what water is to fish. What happens to a fish removed from water?"

In a world designed to capture our attention, remembrance represents a revolutionary reclaiming of consciousness. It redirects awareness toward the only One truly worthy of remembrance, who responds with divine attention:

فَاذْكُرُونِي أَذْكُرْكُمْ

"So remember Me; I will remember you." (2:152)

Let us integrate remembrance into daily life, through morning adhkār, post-prayer practices, Qur'anic recitation, or simply maintaining awareness during ordinary activities. As we do, the Creator remembers us in return, not as an abstract mass but as individual servants, each known by name, each remembered with perfect attention and mercy.

In this reciprocal remembrance lies the profound peace described in the Qur'an:

أَلَا بِذِكْرِ اللَّهِ تَطْمَئِنُّ الْقُلُوبُ

"Truly, in the remembrance of Allah do hearts find rest." (13:28)

Discussion Questions

1. The chapter mentions multiple dimensions of divine remembrance: mercy/forgiveness, protection, guidance, and elevation. Which of these dimensions resonates most strongly with your personal experience of remembering Allah? Can you share a time when you felt one of these dimensions manifesting in your life?
2. Modern life is characterized by constant distraction and fragmented attention. What specific strategies from the chapter could help you create more consistent remembrance in your daily life? Which approach seems most practical for your particular circumstances?
3. The Qur'an warns about those who "forget Allah, so He made them forget themselves." In what ways have you observed this spiritual amnesia in contemporary society or perhaps in your own experience? How might regular remembrance practices protect against this form of forgetfulness?

"O Allah, help me to remember You at all times."

17

The Promise of Temporary Trials

Mogadishu, Somalia

The hospital waiting room was silent except for the rhythmic ticking of the wall clock and the occasional shuffle of papers at the nurse's station. Amina sat motionless, her prayer beads moving silently through her fingers, her lips forming words no one could hear. Forty-eight hours had passed since her seven-year-old son Yusuf had been rushed into emergency surgery after a devastating accident. The doctors had done all they could. Now, they said, it was in Allah's hands.

A woman sat down beside her, Ayah, whom she knew from the local masjid but had never spoken with at length. Ayah placed a gentle hand on Amina's shoulder.

"I lost my daughter three years ago," Ayah said softly. "Different circumstances, same waiting room."

Amina looked up, her eyes hollow with exhaustion and fear. "How did you survive it?" she whispered.

Ayah was quiet for a moment. "I didn't think I would," she finally said. "I questioned everything, my faith, Allah's mercy, the purpose of such pain. But something happened during those darkest days that I never expected. In the complete shattering of my heart, I discovered its infinite capacity."

She reached for Amina's hand. "I'm not here to tell you that everything happens for a reason or that your pain will eventually transform into wisdom, even if that's true. I'm here because I know this path, and no one should walk it alone."

Amina's tears came then, not the controlled, dignified tears she had allowed herself thus far, but deep, body-shaking sobs that seemed to rise from the core of her being. Ayah simply held her, creating a sacred space for grief.

When Amina could speak again, she looked up, her voice barely audible. "The doctors say even if he survives, he might never walk again. I keep asking why Allah would test us this way."

Ayah nodded. "I asked that too. For a long time. But one day, our local imam shared a verse with us that changed everything":

كُلُّ نَفْسٍ ذَائِقَةُ الْمَوْتِ ۗ وَنَبْلُوكُم بِالشَّرِّ وَالْخَيْرِ فِتْنَةً ۖ وَإِلَيْنَا تُرْجَعُونَ

"Every soul will taste death. And We test you [O humanity] with good and evil as a trial, then to Us you will [all] be returned." (21:35)

"He told me something I'll never forget," Ayah continued. "He said, 'Allah doesn't test you to discover what you're made of, He already knows. The test is for you to discover it.'"

The Universality of Trials

The divine promise regarding trials establishes an inescapable reality of human existence: every life will be tested. No one, not even the most beloved of Allah's prophets, is exempt from this universal law. Understanding this fundamentally changes our relationship with hardship. Our trials are not punishments or signs of divine abandonment but part of the shared human journey back to our Creator.

The verse in Surat Al-Anbiyā makes three profound declarations:

1. "Every soul will taste death" - establishing the universality of mortality
2. "We test you with good and evil as a trial" - confirming the comprehensive nature of life's tests
3. "To Us you will all be returned" - affirming the ultimate destination that gives meaning to these tests

This verse informs us that Allah tests His servants with either prosperity or adversity, health or sickness, wealth or poverty, happiness or distress, and similar conditions, to distinguish who will give thanks and who will show patience, both of which are beloved to Allah.

The inclusiveness of this divine testing, through both "good and evil" (بِالشَّرِّ وَالْخَيْرِ), reminds us that even blessings carry responsibilities and challenges. Wealth tests our generosity, health tests our gratitude, knowledge tests our humility, and power tests our justice. Sometimes the trials of ease prove more spiritually dangerous than the trials of hardship.

Personal Stories of Trial

Kareem, a surgeon who had dedicated his life to saving others, found himself on the other side of the operating table after a sudden diagnosis of cancer. "I had spent decades helping patients face mortality," he reflected. "Suddenly, I was confronting my own. My medical knowledge, which had always been my strength, became a source of anxiety as I understood all too well what was happening in my body."

During his treatment, Kareem experienced what he described as "a divine unveiling." "In my weakness, when I couldn't even pray standing up, I discovered a closeness to Allah I had never known in health. My prayers from a hospital bed felt more authentic than those I had performed in the masjid for years. I realized that sometimes Allah breaks us open for us to find what's hidden within."

His experience echoes the wisdom of the Prophet Muhammad ﷺ, who said: "Amazing is the affair of the believer, for all of his affairs are good, and this is for no one except the believer. If something good happens to him, he expresses gratitude, and that is good for him. If something harmful happens to him, he shows patience, and that is good for him."[76]

Grace in Collective Trials

Collective hardships reveal hidden divine wisdom. The 2020 pandemic that isolated millions created unprecedented spiritual connections. Economic crises that stripped material security led many to rediscover faith's unshakable wealth.

As one social worker in Gaza observed: "When bombings intensified and necessities became scarce, artificial barriers between people dissolved. Those with little shared with those who had nothing. In the most severe trial, we witnessed the most beautiful manifestations of faith."

The Prophet's Trials: Finding Strength in Sacred Examples

The trials of the prophets provide both solace and guidance for our own hardships. When we examine their lives, we discover that divine love did not exempt them from suffering but rather entrusted them with tests proportionate to their capacity.

Prophet Muhammad ﷺ, the most beloved to Allah, experienced trials that would break ordinary hearts: the early death of his parents and grandfather, years of persecution, the death of his beloved wife Khadijah and uncle Abu Talib in the same year (known as the Year of Sorrow), the loss of all but one of his children during his lifetime, and assassination attempts that forced him from his homeland.

After the Battle of Uhud, wounded and grieving for the martyrs including his beloved uncle Hamza, he was asked which people are tested most severely. He replied: "The prophets, then those most like them, and then those most like them. A person is tested according to his religious commitment. If his commitment is strong, his test is stronger, and if his religious commitment is weak, he is tested according to his religious commitment. The tribulation will keep affecting the servant until he walks on the earth with no sin on him."[77] This profound teaching transforms our understanding of trials entirely. Far from indicating divine displeasure, they may actually signify divine selection for spiritual elevation.

The Divine Wisdom: Why We Are Tested

Allah's promise regarding trials raises an essential question: Why does an All-Knowing Creator, who already knows what we will do, test us at all?

The answer lies not in Allah's need to discover something unknown, but in our need to discover ourselves. Without trials, certain dimensions of our character and faith would remain theoretical rather than actualized. Trials convert potential into reality, possibility into certainty.

Several divine purposes for trials emerge from Islamic teachings:

1. Revelation of Reality
Trials strip away pretense and reveal our true nature, to ourselves and others. Allah ﷻ states:

أَحَسِبَ النَّاسُ أَن يُتْرَكُوا أَن يَقُولُوا آمَنَّا وَهُمْ لَا يُفْتَنُونَ

"Do people think that they will be left alone because they say: 'We believe' and will not be tested?" (29:2)

This verse identifies the essential role of trials in distinguishing genuine faith from mere verbal claim. Without tests, we might never discover the true depth, or limitation, of our own convictions.

2. Purification and Elevation
Trials function as spiritual purification, removing the heart's attachments to anything other than Allah. The Prophet ﷺ said: "The greatest reward comes with the greatest trial. When Allah loves a people, He tests them. Whoever accepts it earns His pleasure, and whoever shows discontent earns His displeasure."[78] This hadith establishes a direct connection between divine love and trials, suggesting that tests come not as punishment but as opportunity for spiritual advancement.

3. Development of Spiritual Qualities
Certain spiritual virtues can only develop through challenges. Patience emerges through difficulty, gratitude through recognizing blessings amidst hardship, and trust through navigating uncertainty. Without trials, these qualities would remain undeveloped potential rather than living realities in our character.

There are dozens of other examples mentioned in the Qur'an for why trials exist in this temporary world, before the believers experience an eternity of happiness in the afterlife.

Navigating Trials

The promise that trials contain divine purpose doesn't eliminate their difficulty. The pain is real, the challenges substantial. How, then, do we navigate these tests in ways that access their hidden blessings?

1. Embrace the Emotions Without Shame

Islamic spirituality doesn't demand emotional suppression during trials but rather emotional honesty within the framework of ultimate trust. The Prophet ﷺ wept at the death of his son Ibrahim, saying as tears fell from his eyes: "The eyes shed tears, the heart grieves, but we only say what pleases our Lord. O Ibrahim, we are indeed grieved by your departure."[79]

This beautiful example shows that tears and sadness don't contradict submission to Allah's decree but can coexist with it. We need not deny our humanity to affirm our faith.

2. Seek Meaning, Not Just Relief

Our natural instinct during trials is to seek immediate relief. While this is understandable, focusing exclusively on escape from hardship may cause us to miss the growth opportunity within it. Instead, ask reflective questions:

- What might this trial be teaching me about myself?
- Which spiritual muscles is this challenge developing?
- How might this experience be preparing me for future service or understanding?

Yusuf, who spent years managing chronic pain after a serious accident, shared: "Initially, all my prayers were about removing the pain. When I shifted to asking what the pain could teach me, everything changed. I developed empathy I never had before. I discovered patience I didn't know was possible. I learned to value moments of ease I had previously taken for granted."

3. Maintain Spiritual Connection

Trials often disrupt our spiritual routines precisely when we need them most. Maintaining connection with Allah through salah, dhikr, Qur'an, and du'aa provides essential spiritual nutrition during these challenging periods.

Zeina, who cared for her mother through a long battle with dementia, found that abbreviated but consistent worship sustained her better than sporadic but perfect practice: "Some days, all I could manage was a quick prayer and a few verses of Qur'an, but that consistent connection became my lifeline. I learned that Allah doesn't demand perfection during trials, He offers mercy to the consistent heart."

4. Accept Community Support

Islamic tradition emphasizes the community's role in supporting individuals through trials. The Prophet ﷺ described believers: "The example of the believers in their mutual love, mercy, and compassion is like a single body, when one part suffers, the whole body responds with sleeplessness and fever."[80]

Accepting support isn't weakness but acknowledgment of our shared humanity. Sometimes our role is to help; other times, our role is to be helped, and both positions have dignity in the community of faith.

The Promise Beyond the Trial

The final phrase of the verse, "then to Us you will all return," offers the ultimate context for every trial. This promise of return transforms our understanding of hardship by revealing its temporary nature against the backdrop of eternity.

No amount of worry will add anything to what Allah has decreed, but certainty of Allah's mercy and wisdom brings peace in both worlds. This certainty doesn't eliminate pain but provides a horizon beyond it—a promised reunion that gives meaning to every temporary separation, every momentary suffering, every challenge endured with faith.

The Promise That Sustains

My dear brothers and sisters, this divine promise regarding trials doesn't remove their difficulty, but it transforms their meaning. It assures us that our hardships aren't random accidents in an indifferent universe but purposeful tests in a perfectly designed journey back to our Creator.

Every prophet faced trials. Every believer faces trials. What distinguishes us isn't the presence or absence of difficulties but how we encounter them, as meaningless suffering or meaningful opportunities for growth, purification, and elevation.

The trials you face today, whether illness or poverty, loss or abundance, aren't punishments but invitations. Invitations to discover depths of faith you didn't know you possessed, to develop spiritual muscles that only strengthen through resistance, to experience dimensions of divine mercy hidden in times of ease.

These trials are passages, not conclusions. Chapters, not the entire book. And the One who designed these passages promises a return that will transform every trial into testimony, every tear into understanding, every hardship into a step on the journey home.

Discussion Questions

1. Think about a significant trial you've faced or are currently facing. How might reframing it as a divinely designed opportunity for growth rather than random suffering change your experience of it? What specific spiritual qualities might this particular trial be developing in you?
2. The chapter mentions that we are tested through both good and evil. In what ways have times of ease been spiritually challenging for you? How can we maintain taqwā (God-consciousness) during periods of comfort and success?
3. Trials often reveal aspects of ourselves we might not otherwise discover. What have your experiences taught you about yourself—your strengths, limitations, values, or priorities—that you might not have learned any other way?

"O Allah, nothing is easy except what You have made easy, and You make the difficult easy when You wish."

18

The Promise of Consequence

Cairo, Egypt

The afternoon prayer had just concluded at the masjid when Imam Fareed noticed Zayn lingering behind, his young face troubled. At twenty-six, Zayn had recently returned to the faith after years of distance. His journey back had been precipitated by a series of personal crises, such as addiction issues, broken relationships, and finally, a health scare that had forced him to reassess his life choices.

"Something on your mind, brother?" the imam inquired gently.

Zayn hesitated before speaking. "I've been thinking about the connection between my past choices and the difficulties I'm facing now. Some brothers suggested that my problems are direct punishments from Allah for my sins." His voice lowered. "Is that how it works? Is Allah punishing me for everything I did wrong?"

Imam Fareed considered the question carefully. "Allah's relationship with us is more profound than simple punishment," he began. "Let me share a verse that offers insight into this matter:"

ظَهَرَ الْفَسَادُ فِي الْبَرِّ وَالْبَحْرِ بِمَا كَسَبَتْ أَيْدِي النَّاسِ لِيُذِيقَهُم بَعْضَ
الَّذِي عَمِلُوا لَعَلَّهُمْ يَرْجِعُونَ

"Corruption has spread on land and sea as a result of what people's hands have done, so that Allah may cause them to taste [the consequences of] some of their deeds and perhaps they might return [to the Right Path]." (30:41)

The imam explained, "This verse reveals a divine promise regarding consequences in this world, not as mere punishment, but as an invitation to return to Allah. Notice three crucial points: First, we taste only 'some' consequences, not all, a mercy in itself. Second, these consequences have a purpose, to guide us back to the right path. Third, there's an inherent optimism in the phrase 'perhaps they might return'—an expectation of positive response."

As understanding dawned in Zayn's eyes, the imam continued, "Your difficulties aren't simply punishment; they're an opportunity for growth and return. The question isn't just 'Why is this happening to me?' but 'What is this teaching me, and how can I grow closer to Allah through it?'"

The Natural Law of Consequence

The Qur'anic promise of worldly consequences for sin reflects a profound reality: Allah has established natural laws that govern the relationship between our actions and their outcomes. This isn't arbitrary punishment but the operation of divine wisdom through consistent patterns of cause and effect.

Another verse clarifies this relationship on a personal level:

وَمَا أَصَابَكُم مِّن مُّصِيبَةٍ فَبِمَا كَسَبَتْ أَيْدِيكُمْ وَيَعْفُو عَن كَثِيرٍ

"Whatever affliction befalls you is because of what your own hands have committed. And He pardons much." (42:30)

This verse establishes three critical principles:

1. Causality - There exists a causal relationship between our actions and their outcomes
2. Responsibility - We bear personal responsibility for the consequences of our choices
3. Mercy - Allah pardons much, sparing us from many potential consequences

Allah is more merciful to His servants than to punish them for every sin they commit. What afflictions do reach them are the result of some of their sins, and Allah pardons much more than that. This understanding transforms our perspective on hardship from simple punishment to a complex interplay of natural consequences, divine wisdom, and mercy.

The Categories of Worldly Consequences

Islamic scholars have identified several ways that sins generate consequences in this world:

1. Direct Natural Consequences: Many sins carry inherent negative outcomes—substance abuse leads to health deterioration, dishonesty destroys trust, exploitation creates systemic injustice. These follow naturally from the actions themselves.

2. Societal Consequences: Collective sins generate broader impacts. Environmental degradation, family breakdown, and economic inequality result from abandoning divine guidance on community and stewardship.

3. Spiritual Consequences: The Prophet ﷺ said: "When a servant commits a sin, a dark spot appears on his heart."[81] This results in hardened hearts, diminished spiritual joy, and decreased moral sensitivity.

The Mercy Within Consequence

Partial consequences only: We taste only "some" of our actions' consequences. For every consequence experienced, countless others are averted by divine forbearance.

Educational purpose: The phrase "perhaps they might return" reveals consequences serve growth rather than pure punishment—guiding toward positive change.

Expiation: The Prophet ﷺ taught that worldly difficulties reduce accountability in the Hereafter: "No fatigue, illness, or anxiety afflicts a Muslim, even the prick of a thorn, but Allah expiates some sins by it."[82]

Contemporary Examples of Collective Consequences

While individual sins have personal impacts, collective departure from divine guidance produces widespread consequences that affect entire societies.

Environmental Degradation

The Qur'anic reference to corruption appearing "on land and sea" finds striking fulfillment in contemporary environmental crises. Climate change, pollution, species extinction, and resource depletion directly result from exploitative approaches to the natural world that contradict the Islamic principle of stewardship (khilāfah).

Social Fragmentation

The breakdown of family structures, rising isolation, and mental health crises reflect consequences of abandoning divine guidance on human relationships. When societies prioritize individual gratification over mutual responsibility and immediate desires over enduring commitments, the social fabric inevitably frays.

Economic Inequality

Systems built on interest (ribā), exploitation, and materialistic values produce the extreme inequality witnessed globally. When wealth concentrates among the few while billions struggle for necessities, we see a direct consequence of disregarding Islamic economic principles:

- Prohibition of interest
- Obligation of zakat
- Encouragement of charitable giving
- Ethical restrictions on business practices

Personal Consequences as Invitations to Return

Mahmoud, after years of pursuing wealth through questionable means, experienced a business collapse that left him devastated. "Initially, I was angry at my fate," he recalled.

"But I recognized patterns connecting my choices to outcomes. The collapse wasn't arbitrary punishment, it was the accumulated result of my path, and simultaneously an invitation to choose differently."

This recognition transformed his suffering into meaningful growth. "My difficulties became stepping stones toward a more authentic life."

The Path Through Consequence to Restoration

When facing consequences of sin, whether personal or collective, the Islamic response involves several key elements:

1. Recognition: Take honest ownership of choices that contributed to the situation, creating the foundation for change.

2. Sincere Repentance: "The one who repents from sin is like one who has no sin."[83] This includes stopping the sin, feeling genuine remorse, intending never to return, and making amends where possible.

3. Patient Perseverance: Consequences often remain after repentance. Trust Allah's timing while working toward positive change. "Indeed, with hardship comes ease" (94:5).

4. Constructive Action: "Allah will not change the condition of a people until they change what is in themselves" (13:11).

The Promise That Guides and Restores

The divine promise regarding worldly consequences represents profound mercy disguised as difficulty. By establishing natural laws that bring a portion of our actions' consequences into earthly experience, Allah provides:

1. Tangible feedback that guides our choices
2. Opportunities for recognition and return before the final reckoning
3. Means of purification that lightens our account in the Hereafter

Let us return to Zayn. Six months later, he shared: "Understanding my difficulties as invitations rather than punishments transformed everything. The health issues became motivation to care for my body. Broken relationships revealed patterns I needed to change. Even financial struggles forced me to reevaluate priorities."

"The consequences didn't disappear overnight," he added. "But they've become a path toward Allah rather than punishment from Him. That makes all the difference."

This transformation represents the purpose of worldly consequences, not to punish but to guide us back to our Creator, the source of healing and restoration.

Discussion Questions

1. Reflect on a difficulty you've experienced that might connect to previous choices or actions. How might reframing this experience as an "invitation to return" rather than a "punishment" change your approach to addressing it?
2. The chapter mentions that we taste only "some" consequences of our actions in this world, with Allah pardoning much more. How might this perspective of divine mercy affect your understanding of both the difficulties and blessings in your life?
3. Consider the broader societal consequences discussed in the chapter (environmental, social, economic). What personal responsibility might you bear in contributing to or alleviating these collective challenges? What specific actions could you take to be part of the solution rather than the problem?

"Our Lord, give us good in this world and good in the next world, and save us from the punishment of the Fire."

19

The Promise of Return

Gaza, Palestine

The autumn rain fell softly as Hamzah stood motionless before his father's fresh grave. At seventy-three, his father had seemed invincible, a retired professor whose intellect remained razor-sharp until the sudden heart attack that took him three days ago. Now, as mourners dispersed, Hamzah remained, unable to reconcile this moment's finality with the memories of his father's voice, laughter, and wisdom.

A hand gently touched his shoulder. It was Imam Khattab, an elderly scholar who had known Hamzah's family for decades.

"When my own father passed," the imam said quietly, "I stood exactly where you stand now, asking the same unspoken questions I see in your eyes."

Hamzah turned, his face lined with grief. "I knew this day would come," he whispered. "We all know death is certain. Yet somehow..." His voice broke. "I wasn't ready."

The imam nodded, understanding etched in the lines of his weathered face. "None of us truly are. But your father, may Allah have mercy on him, lived with beautiful awareness of this moment's inevitability."

He gestured toward the rows of graves stretching across the hillside, some centuries old, others freshly dug. "Your father once told me that he visited this cemetery every month, not out of morbidity but clarity. He said it was his most important appointment, the one that kept all other appointments in perspective."

The imam's eyes grew distant with memory as he continued:

"He would quote Al-Hasan al-Basri: 'May Allah have mercy on the man who works for the likes of this day; for today you are able to do what these brothers of yours, the residents of these graves, cannot do.'"

Something shifted in Hamzah's heart as these words penetrated his grief. His father had indeed lived with remarkable intentionality, prioritizing relationships over acquisition, forgiveness over resentment, worship over distraction. Perhaps his father's greatest legacy wasn't his academic achievements but his conscious preparation for this very moment.

As they walked slowly from the graveyard, the imam recited softly:

كُلُّ مَنْ عَلَيْهَا فَانٍ وَيَبْقَىٰ وَجْهُ رَبِّكَ ذُو الْجَلَالِ وَالْإِكْرَامِ

"Every being on earth is bound to perish. Only your Lord Himself, full of Majesty and Honor, will remain [forever]." (55:26-27)

These ancient words, recited countless times through fourteen centuries, suddenly felt intensely personal to Hamzah, as if they had been revealed precisely for this moment, this loss, this awakening.

The Most Certain Promise

Among all divine promises, death stands unique in its absolute certainty and universal application. While other promises may manifest differently across individual lives, the promise of mortality touches every human being without exception. Allah states with characteristic clarity:

وَاللَّهُ خَلَقَكُمْ ثُمَّ يَتَوَفَّاكُمْ ۚ وَمِنكُم مَّن يُرَدُّ إِلَىٰ أَرْذَلِ الْعُمُرِ لِكَيْ لَا يَعْلَمَ بَعْدَ عِلْمٍ شَيْئًا ۚ إِنَّ اللَّهَ عَلِيمٌ قَدِيرٌ

"Allah has created you, and then causes you to die. And some of you are left to reach the most feeble stage of life so that they may know nothing after having known much. Indeed, Allah is All-Knowing, Most Capable." (16:70)

This verse frames human existence as a complete journey—from creation to death, with some experiencing the full arc of life into advanced age and diminishing capacity. The divine promise embedded here isn't merely that we will die, but that our entire life trajectory falls within Allah's perfect knowledge and power.

The companion verse in Surat Ar-Raḥmān emphasizes the comprehensive nature of this promise:

كُلُّ مَنْ عَلَيْهَا فَانٍ وَيَبْقَىٰ وَجْهُ رَبِّكَ ذُو الْجَلَالِ وَالْإِكْرَامِ

"Every being on earth is bound to perish. Only your Lord Himself, full of Majesty and Honor, will remain [forever]." (55:26-27)

The word "fān" (فَانٍ) describes not just death but perishing, vanishing, coming to nothing. It conveys the complete temporal nature of everything in creation contrasted with the eternal reality of the Creator. This isn't merely information, it's revelation that reorients our entire existence when truly comprehended.

When Tomorrow Never Comes

Hind's voice trembled as she shared her story with the women's circle. At thirty-four, she was the youngest widow among them, her husband having died suddenly during his morning jog six months earlier.

"Ahmad and I had our lives perfectly planned," she explained. "We were saving for a bigger house, postponing having children until we were more financially secure, putting off the Hajj journey until we had more vacation time. We lived entirely for a future that he never saw."

Her eyes filled with tears. "The morning he died was ordinary in every way. He kissed me goodbye, said he'd pick up groceries on his way home from work, and left for his run. That quick goodbye was our last conversation—no profound final words, no awareness that everything was about to change forever."

Hind paused, gathering herself. "What haunts me isn't just losing him but realizing how much life we postponed. All those conversations we would have 'someday,' all those experiences we delayed, all those chances to worship together we let slip by, assuming tomorrow would always come."

Her story pierces the illusion that many of us maintain, that death is a distant appointment rather than an ever-present possibility. The Prophet ﷺ addressed this directly: "Remember frequently the destroyer of pleasures [death]."[84]

This remembrance isn't meant to cast a shadow over life's joys but to infuse them with deeper appreciation and purpose. When we recognize each day as a potentially final gift, ordinary moments transform into precious opportunities.

The Forgotten Wisdom

Modern society distances itself from death's reality, hospitals replace home deathbeds, creating the illusion death can be indefinitely postponed. This deprives us of wisdom from regular confrontation with mortality.

As one chaplain observed: "Previous generations witnessed natural life progression at home. Today, many reach adulthood without seeing death, creating spiritual disability—inability to grasp life's most fundamental reality."

The Prophet ﷺ advised: "Visit the graves, for they remind you of the Hereafter,"[85] a spiritual medicine for the forgetfulness that leads to misplaced priorities.

The Time We Have Been Given

Imagine finding an envelope containing a bank statement for an account in your name. Upon opening it, you discover that each morning, exactly 86,400 seconds are deposited into your account. By day's end, whatever you haven't used disappears, it can't be saved, transferred, or carried forward. The next morning, another 86,400 seconds appear.

How would you manage this precious, perishable resource? Would you spend it carelessly on matters of no lasting value? Would you allow others to squander it on your behalf? Or would you invest it in what truly matters, knowing each day's amount might be your last deposit?

This metaphor, while imperfect, captures something essential about time, the one resource that, once spent, can never be recovered. The Prophet ﷺ emphasized this when he informed us that the believer will not move on the Day of Judgment (from accountability) until they are asked about five matters, starting with: their lifetime and how they spent it.[86]

This accountability for our time elevates ordinary choices to spiritual significance. How we spend our hours isn't merely a matter of personal preference but sacred stewardship.

When Strength Becomes Weakness

Allah's reference to those reaching "the most feeble stage of life" where they "know nothing after having known much" describes severe cognitive decline.

Dr. Hatem, a neurologist, shared a personal story: "My patient, a Qur'an memorizer who couldn't recognize family, would complete verses his son began reciting. Something deeper than conscious memory remained—as if the Qur'an was written on his heart itself."

This teaches humility about our temporary capabilities and hope about what truly endures. When intellect and independence fade, the soul's connection to Allah, cultivated through lifetime worship, remains.

Death's Hidden Mercies

While we naturally fear death and grieve those we lose, Islamic tradition recognizes death as containing profound mercies alongside its apparent harshness. Consider these dimensions of divine wisdom within mortality:

1. The Ultimate Equalizer

The Prophet ﷺ one time passed by a funeral and said: Either he is at rest, or others are at rest from him." They asked: "O Messenger of Allah, what does it mean for someone to be at rest, and for others to be at rest from him?"

He replied: "The believing servant is at rest from the toil and harm of this world, having moved on to the mercy of Allah. But the wicked servant — people, the land, the trees, and the animals find rest from him."[87] In the grave, there's no distinction between rich and poor, only the quality of one's relationship with Allah remains. And the evil person who departs relieves the living from their oppression and evil.

2. The End of Tyranny

Throughout human history, countless people have suffered under oppressive powers that seemed invincible. For the oppressed, death represents not only their own release but the certain knowledge that their oppressors will follow. No tyrant, no matter how powerful, escapes this divine appointment.

Allah reminded the Pharaoh of this reality through Moses ﷺ:

قَالَ رَبُّنَا الَّذِي أَعْطَىٰ كُلَّ شَيْءٍ خَلْقَهُ ثُمَّ هَدَىٰ

"Our Lord is He who gave everything its form, then guided it." (20:50)

This guidance includes the path to death, which no creature, not even the most powerful ruler, can avoid. For believers suffering under oppression throughout history, this certainty has provided profound consolation.

3. The Gateway to Divine Justice

In a world where justice often fails, where criminals escape punishment and victims go without vindication, death serves as the gateway to ultimate accountability.

Allah ﷻ reminds us in the Qur'an:

وَنَضَعُ الْمَوَازِينَ الْقِسْطَ لِيَوْمِ الْقِيَامَةِ فَلَا تُظْلَمُ نَفْسٌ شَيْئًا ۖ
وَإِن كَانَ مِثْقَالَ حَبَّةٍ مِّنْ خَرْدَلٍ أَتَيْنَا بِهَا ۗ وَكَفَىٰ بِنَا حَاسِبِينَ

"We will set up the scales of justice for the Day of Judgment, so no soul will be wronged in the least. Even if a deed is the weight of a mustard seed, We will bring it forth. And sufficient are We as reckoners." (21:47)

Without death and the judgment that follows, injustice would have the final word in countless human stories. The promise of mortality thus contains within it the greater promise that every oppressed person will receive justice, every hidden good will be revealed, and every secret wrong will be exposed.

Living Before We Die

The ultimate purpose of contemplating death isn't to induce fear or depression but to awaken us to life's precious opportunity before it passes. Consider these transformative approaches to living in light of mortality:

1. Reconcile Now: The Prophet ﷺ forbade Muslims from remaining estranged for more than three nights.[88] Life is too short for prolonged estrangement.
2. Prioritize What Endures: "When a person dies, their deeds cease except for three: ongoing charity, beneficial knowledge, or a righteous child who prays for them."[89] Invest in what continues beyond the grave.
3. Daily Accountability: Take account of yourselves before you are taken to account. Each day, ask: If today were my last, what would I present to Allah?

This practice of self-accountability transforms ordinary moments into opportunities for spiritual growth. Imagine each evening reviewing the day with these questions:

- If today were my last, what would I be proud to present to Allah?
- What actions today might I regret if I could not correct them tomorrow?
- How did I invest or waste the precious hours I was given?

This regular reflection, inspired by death's certainty, creates life of exceptional intentionality and meaning.

The Promise That Completes All Promises

Allah's promise of death frames all His other promises. It gives urgency to His warnings, sweetness to His mercy, and context to every joy and sorrow.

Nine months after his father's funeral, Hamzah was completing a project his father had started, compiling the family history. He discovered his father's journal with this final entry:

"I visited the cemetery again today. Death has become not a stranger to fear but a teacher to respect. It taught me to love more deeply, forgive more quickly, worship sincerely, prioritize wisely. If acknowledging death's certainty has given this much meaning to my life, perhaps death itself will give meaning to everything else."

Hamzah closed the journal, tears flowing. His father's final gift wasn't just how to live, but how to face the promise awaiting us all. In embracing this divine certainty rather than denying it, his father discovered life's deepest secret: conscious mortality leads not to despair but to extraordinary presence and purpose in each precious moment.

May Allah grant us wisdom to live aware of His final promise, courage to prepare for our inevitable meeting with Him, and faith to recognize that what appears as an ending is, for the believer, the most beautiful beginning.

Discussion Questions

1. Reflect on a time when awareness of mortality brought greater meaning or clarity to your life. How might you incorporate healthy remembrance of death into your regular spiritual practice?
2. Our modern society tends to distance us from death and aging, treating them as aberrations rather than natural parts of the human journey. How has this affected your own perspective on mortality? What traditional practices or viewpoints mentioned in the chapter might help restore a healthier relationship with life's final stage?
3. The Prophet ﷺ taught that a person's deeds continue after death through ongoing charity, beneficial knowledge, or righteous children who pray for them. Which of these pathways resonates most with you personally, and what specific steps might you take to establish this enduring legacy?

"O Allah, make the best of my life its end, the best of my deeds their conclusion, and the best of my days the day I meet You."

20

The Promise of Mercy at Death

Khartoum, Sudan

The hospital room was quiet except for the rhythmic beeping of monitors and the soft, labored breathing of Shaykh Abu Ammar. At ninety-seven, the beloved teacher who had guided generations of students through the intricacies of Islamic knowledge was making his final journey. His family had gathered, their faces etched with the complex emotions that accompany impending loss—grief mingled with resignation, pain softened by faith.

Yet something in the room seemed at odds with the somber occasion. The dying scholar's face, despite his physical discomfort, held an inexplicable peace. Occasionally, a gentle smile would touch his lips, as if he were witnessing something beautiful beyond the perception of those around him.

His granddaughter Noura, a medical student who had been keeping vigil by his bedside, leaned forward as he whispered something. The family drew closer.

"I see them," the shaykh murmured, his voice surprisingly clear.

"See what, grandpa?" Noura asked gently, wondering if medication was causing hallucinations.

"The merciful ones," he replied with quiet certainty. "Just as Allah promised. I'm not afraid." He closed his eyes briefly, the smile deepening.

His son, Dr. Khabbab, looked at Noura. As a physician, he recognized the signs of approaching death. As a believer, he recognized something else: the manifestation of a divine promise his father had spent a lifetime preparing to receive.

Shaykh Abu Ammar opened his eyes once more, looking not at his family but slightly above them. "La ilaha illa Allah," he whispered. With these final words of testimony, his chest rose and fell one last time.

In the profound silence that followed, Khabbab recited quietly:

إِنَّ الَّذِينَ قَالُوا رَبُّنَا اللَّهُ ثُمَّ اسْتَقَامُوا تَتَنَزَّلُ عَلَيْهِمُ الْمَلَائِكَةُ
أَلَّا تَخَافُوا وَلَا تَحْزَنُوا وَأَبْشِرُوا بِالْجَنَّةِ الَّتِي كُنتُمْ تُوعَدُونَ

"Surely those who say, 'Our Lord is Allah,' and then remain steadfast, the angels descend upon them, saying, 'Do not fear, nor grieve. Rather, rejoice in the good news of Paradise, which you have been promised.'" (41:30)

The Most Beautiful Departure

Among the countless divine promises in the Qur'an, perhaps none offers more profound comfort than the assurance of angelic presence and divine mercy at the moment of death for those who have lived with steadfast faith. This extraordinary guarantee transforms what might otherwise be a moment of terror and uncertainty into one of transcendent peace and joyful anticipation.

The verse in Surat Fuṣṣilat presents this promise with exquisite clarity and beauty. This verse continues, revealing even more about this divine blessing:

نَحْنُ أَوْلِيَاؤُكُمْ فِي الْحَيَاةِ الدُّنْيَا وَفِي الْآخِرَةِ ۖ وَلَكُمْ فِيهَا مَا تَشْتَهِي أَنفُسُكُمْ وَلَكُمْ فِيهَا مَا تَدَّعُونَ

"We [angels] were your guardians in the worldly life and [will be] in the Hereafter. And you will have therein whatever your souls desire, and you will have therein whatever you request [or wish for]." (41:31)

The culmination of this beautiful passage reveals the source of these blessings:

نُزُلًا مِّنْ غَفُورٍ رَّحِيمٍ

"An accommodation from the All-Forgiving, Most Merciful [Lord]." (41:32)

These verses weave together a comprehensive picture of the believer's final moments and beyond—angels descending with comfort and glad tidings, serving as guardians throughout the journey, and all of this flowing from Allah's boundless mercy and forgiveness.

Understanding True Steadfastness

The profound comfort described in these verses isn't promised to everyone who identifies as Muslim, but specifically to "those who say, 'Our Lord is Allah,' and then remain steadfast." This qualification—steadfastness (istiqāmah)—merits deep reflection. What exactly constitutes the steadfastness that earns such a beautiful departure?

The early Muslim authorities (salaf) offered profound insights into this concept. From their explanations, we discover that true steadfastness encompasses several interrelated dimensions:

1. Consistency in Monotheism
Abu Bakr (ra) said: They are those who did not equate Him with anything else (i.e., by committing shirk). 'Umar ibn al-Khaṭṭāb (ra) emphasized that the steadfast are "those who remained firm in their obedience to Allah, not running about like foxes."[90] This vivid imagery suggests consistency and stability in one's devotion, rather than flitting between commitment and negligence.

2. Sincerity of Intention
Uthmān ibn 'Affān (ra) highlighted that steadfastness includes "performing deeds purely for Allah's sake."[91] This reminds us that external conformity without internal sincerity falls short of true istiqāmah.

3. Comprehensive Obedience
Ali ibn Abi Talib reported from Ibn 'Abbas that this verse emphasized "the faithful performance of duties enjoined by Allah."[92] This points to the practical dimension of steadfastness, following through on divine commands across all aspects of life.

These explanations reveal something profound: istiqāmah isn't merely perseverance but a holistic state that encompasses belief, intention, and action maintained consistently throughout life.

As Ibn Rajab al-Hanbali observed centuries later: "Those who say 'Our Lord is Allah' are many, but those who practice with steadfastness are fewer in number."[93] His observation remains painfully relevant today, challenging us to examine whether we fall among the many who claim faith or the fewer who embody steadfast commitment.

Al-Ḥasan al-Baṣrī, when he would recite this verse, would say: "O Allah, You are our Lord, so grant us steadfastness."[94]

The Angels' Three-Part Promise

For those who achieve this comprehensive steadfastness, the angelic promise offers three specific comforts:

1. "Do Not Fear"
The first angelic assurance addresses the natural human fear of the unknown, particularly the uncertainty of what follows death. This fear, which can overwhelm even the strongest individuals, dissolves in the face of direct angelic reassurance. The angels essentially say, "There is no need to fear what lies ahead, for you are headed toward divine mercy, not punishment."

2. "Do Not Grieve"
The second assurance addresses grief over what is being left behind—family, unfulfilled plans, unfinished work. The angels comfort the departing soul, assuring them that whatever they leave behind is being exchanged for something incomparably better. This doesn't negate the natural sadness of separation but places it in the context of a greater reunion.

3. "Rejoice in the Good News of Paradise"
Beyond merely removing fear and grief, the angels actively invite the believer to positive joy, to anticipate the paradise they have been promised. This transforms the moment of death from an ending to be dreaded into a homecoming to be celebrated.

This three-part promise creates a complete emotional transformation for the believer at life's end, removing negative emotions (fear and grief) while introducing positive anticipation (joy). No wonder those who witness the deaths of the righteous often report seeing inexplicable peace or even happiness on their faces.

The Angels as Guardians Through the Journey

The divine promise extends beyond the moment of death to encompass ongoing angelic companionship. The angels declare:

نَحْنُ أَوْلِيَاؤُكُمْ فِي الْحَيَاةِ الدُّنْيَا وَفِي الْآخِرَةِ

"We [angels] were your guardians in the worldly life and [will be] in the Hereafter." (41:31)

This remarkable statement reveals something many believers may not fully appreciate: the angels who bring comfort at death aren't strangers but long-time companions who have been with us throughout our lives. The angels say, "We were your companions in the worldly life, and we will be your companions until you enter Jannah (Paradise)."

This ongoing guardianship encompasses several stages of the believer's journey:

1. During Earthly Life
The angels serve as unseen protectors and supporters throughout the believer's life. Allah confirms:

لَهُ مُعَقِّبَاتٌ مِّن بَيْنِ يَدَيْهِ وَمِنْ خَلْفِهِ يَحْفَظُونَهُ مِنْ أَمْرِ اللَّهِ

"For each [person] there are successive [angels] before and behind him who protect him by the decree of Allah." (13:11)

These guardian angels record our deeds, seek forgiveness for us, and protect us according to Allah's decree. While invisible to us, they remain constant companions through every moment of our lives.

2. At the Moment of Death

The angels who have witnessed our struggles and devotion throughout life are the same ones who descend with glad tidings at death. Their presence represents not just momentary comfort but the culmination of a lifelong relationship.

3. During Al-Barzakh (The Intermediate State)

The angels continue their guardianship through the period between death and resurrection, ensuring the believer's comfort in the grave.

The Prophet ﷺ described how the righteous soul is carried by the angels and welcomed in the heavens after death, indicating ongoing angelic care during this intermediate state.

4. On the Day of Resurrection

The angels will continue to support believers through the challenges of the Day of Judgment. Allah describes how:

وَتَتَلَقَّاهُمُ الْمَلَائِكَةُ هَٰذَا يَوْمُكُمُ الَّذِي كُنتُمْ تُوعَدُونَ

"And the angels will meet them, [saying], 'This is your Day which you have been promised.'" (21:103)

5. Entry into Paradise

The final stage of angelic guardianship concludes with escorting believers into Paradise:

وَالْمَلَائِكَةُ يَدْخُلُونَ عَلَيْهِم مِّن كُلِّ بَابٍ سَلَامٌ عَلَيْكُم بِمَا صَبَرْتُمْ ۚ فَنِعْمَ عُقْبَى الدَّارِ

"And the angels will enter upon them from every gate, [saying], 'Peace be upon you for what you patiently endured. And excellent is the final home.'" (13:23-24)

This comprehensive guardianship reveals that believers are never alone in their journey, from the first moment of faith to the final entry into eternal bliss, angelic companions remain present, though usually unseen.

Paradise as Divine Hospitality

The conclusion of this magnificent promise reveals something extraordinary about the nature of Paradise itself:

نُزُلًا مِّنْ غَفُورٍ رَّحِيمٍ

"An accommodation from the All-Forgiving, Most Merciful [Lord]." (41:32)

The Arabic word نُزُلًا (nuzulan) refers specifically to honored hospitality, the generous accommodation prepared for a valued guest. This reveals that Paradise isn't merely a reward dispensed according to strict justice but a lavish expression of divine generosity and welcome.

Even more significantly, this hospitality comes explicitly from Allah as "the All-Forgiving, Most Merciful." These particular divine names—Al-Ghafur (الْغَفُور) and Ar-Raheem (الرَّحِيم), remind us that Paradise is ultimately a matter of forgiveness and mercy rather than earned entitlement.

As the Prophet ﷺ taught: "No one will enter Paradise by virtue of their deeds alone." When his companions asked, "Not even you, O Messenger of Allah?" he replied: "Not even me, unless Allah covers me with His mercy and grace."[95]

This understanding transforms our relationship with good deeds. While steadfastness and righteous actions are essential prerequisites for Paradise, they function not as currency to purchase divine favor but as expressions of love and submission that attract divine mercy. Paradise remains fundamentally a gift that far exceeds what any human could earn through deeds alone.

Glimpses of the Promise

Throughout Islamic history, believers have witnessed remarkable signs of this divine promise fulfilled at the deathbeds of the righteous. Consider these accounts:

Bilal ibn Rabah, the beloved companion and first official caller to prayer of Islam, spoke his final words with extraordinary joy: "Tomorrow we shall meet the beloved—Muhammad and his companions!"[96]

Even today, some hospice workers share first-hand stories of devout Muslims who die with exceptional serenity. As one nurse observed: "Many cases I've seen seem to experience a moment of recognition and peace just before death, as if sensing something invisible to us."

Living for a Beautiful Ending

The promise of angelic comfort and divine mercy at death isn't merely information about the future but guidance for the present. It invites us to shape our lives around securing this beautiful ending. Consider these practical implications:

1. Prioritize Steadfastness: Maintain pure monotheism, commit to Islam entirely, keep clear moral boundaries, develop consistency in worship.

2. Strengthen Angelic Relationships: Maintain ritual purity, create welcoming environments through Qur'an and dhikr, avoid what repels angels.

3. Balance Fear and Hope: Work diligently while trusting divine mercy, take account of shortcomings while maintaining optimism.

4. Let Death Motivate Life: Each act of worship becomes preparation for angelic glad tidings, each resistance to temptation secures divine guardianship.

The Promise That Changes Everything

Allah's promise of angelic comfort at death transforms death's meaning, from terrifying end into joyful homecoming, from final separation into ultimate reunion.

This promise makes every struggle for steadfastness worthwhile. Every prayer maintained despite fatigue, every charity given despite pressure, every temptation resisted, all contribute to securing this beautiful ending.

For the steadfast, death becomes not when everything is lost, but when everything is finally gained. Not when loved ones are left behind, but when the Most Beloved is finally met. Not when darkness falls, but when true light finally dawns.

Let us live conscious of this promise, striving for the steadfastness it requires while trusting in the mercy it guarantees. When our final moments arrive, may we too experience the descent of angels with their beautiful tidings: "Do not fear, nor grieve. Rather, rejoice in the good news of Paradise."

Discussion Questions

1. The chapter emphasizes that true steadfastness (istiqāmah) encompasses belief, intention, and action maintained consistently throughout life. In which of these areas do you find maintaining steadfastness most challenging, and what practical steps might help strengthen this aspect of your faith?
2. Reflect on the three-part angelic promise: "Do not fear, nor grieve. Rather, rejoice in the good news of Paradise." Which of these three assurances speaks most powerfully to you personally, and why? How might keeping this specific comfort in mind influence your daily life?
3. The passage describes Paradise as "an accommodation from the All-Forgiving, Most Merciful [Lord]," suggesting it is fundamentally a gift of mercy rather than something earned through deeds alone. How does this understanding influence your approach to religious obligations and spiritual striving?

"O Allah, make the best of my provisions taqwā (God-consciousness), and make my return to Your mercy."

PROMISES FOR THE AFTERLIFE

21

The Promise of the Hereafter

The Promise That Changes Everything

In the tapestry of divine promises, one stands out with particular urgency—the promise of an afterlife and the warning against worldly deception. Allah addresses all of humanity with this fundamental truth:

يَٰٓأَيُّهَا ٱلنَّاسُ إِنَّ وَعْدَ ٱللَّهِ حَقٌّ ۖ فَلَا تَغُرَّنَّكُمُ ٱلْحَيَوٰةُ ٱلدُّنْيَا ۖ وَلَا يَغُرَّنَّكُم بِٱللَّهِ ٱلْغَرُورُ

"O humanity! Indeed, Allah's promise is true. So do not let the life of this world deceive you, nor let the Chief Deceiver deceive you about Allah." (35:5)

The Universal Call

Notice how this verse begins—not with "O believers" but with "O humanity." This comprehensive call transcends all barriers of time, place, culture, and belief. The message that follows isn't restricted to those who already believe; it extends to every human being who has ever lived or will ever live. This universal address underscores a profound truth: the reality of the afterlife isn't merely a religious doctrine but a fundamental truth concerning the very nature of our existence.

When Allah declares that His promise is true, He speaks of something more real and certain than the ground beneath our feet. The word *ḥaqq* doesn't suggest probability or possibility—it denotes absolute truth, a reality more solid than the physical world we perceive. This promise refers primarily to the Hereafter, that inevitable moment when all affairs will be presented before our Creator, when the veils of this temporal existence fall away to reveal what was always real.

The Art of Deception

The verse then unveils a dual warning that strikes at the heart of human vulnerability. First, it cautions against the deceptive nature of worldly life itself, then it warns of the deceptions whispered by Satan. These aren't separate threats but intertwined realities that work together to cloud our spiritual vision.

Consider how the world deceives us. It doesn't merely exist in a misleading state—the Arabic word *taghurrannakum* implies active deception, as if the world itself conspires to maintain illusions that distance us from eternal truth. This deception manifests in countless ways, each more subtle than the last. The world whispers that it is permanent when it is fleeting, that it is the ultimate reality when it is merely a shadow, that success here guarantees success hereafter when the two may have no correlation at all.

Walk through any city, scroll through any social media feed, or sit in any gathering, and you'll witness this deception at work. The relentless pursuit of material accumulation, the endless comparison with others' worldly achievements, the gnawing anxiety about temporal matters that will seem laughably insignificant in a hundred years, let alone in the eternal scope of the Hereafter. The world creates an illusion of permanence so convincing that we often forget we're merely travelers passing through.

The Master of Illusion

The second warning introduces us to al-gharur, the Chief Deceiver himself—Satan, whose deceptions about Allah are even more sophisticated than the world's material distractions. His strategies have evolved with the times while maintaining their essential nature. In our age, he no longer needs to convince most people to bow before idols of stone. Instead, he promotes subtler forms of denial: the notion that if God exists, He must be too distant to care about human affairs, or that divine mercy is so expansive it requires no accountability, or that morality is entirely subjective and disconnected from any transcendent source.

These contemporary deceptions wear the masks of intellectual sophistication. They come dressed as philosophical materialism that reduces all existence to mere atoms and void, as secular humanism that places humanity at the center while denying our connection to the Divine, or as a vague spirituality that acknowledges some higher power while rejecting the guidance that power has provided. The Chief Deceiver has become remarkably adept at using our own intelligence and education against us, turning the very tools meant to lead us to truth into instruments of confusion.

Living Between Two Worlds

Understanding this reality doesn't call for withdrawal from the world. The early scholars spoke of *zuhd*, often translated as asceticism, but more accurately understood as leaving behind what doesn't benefit us in the next life. This doesn't mean abandoning our families, careers, or communities. Rather, it means engaging with all these things while maintaining a profound awareness of their temporary nature. It's the difference between holding something in your hand and not letting it hold your heart.

Imagine a traveler staying at a hotel. They use the amenities, rest in comfort, perhaps even enjoy the luxury, but they never forget they're just passing through. They don't invest in renovating the room or become devastated when checkout time arrives. This is how believers are called to engage with the world, fully present but never attached, participating without being possessed by participation itself.

This balanced approach transforms how we view everything. Time becomes not merely something to fill but a finite resource to invest in eternal returns. Our relationships are valued not just for their worldly benefits but for how they strengthen our connection to the Divine and our preparation for the Hereafter. Our resources—money, knowledge, influence—are seen as trusts to be used wisely, knowing we'll be asked about every blessing we received and how we used it.

The Question That Changes Everything

All of this leads to a question that should echo in our hearts daily: "What have I prepared for my meeting with Allah?" Not what have I accumulated, achieved, or acquired in worldly terms, but what have I prepared for that inevitable moment when all veils drop and we stand before our Creator?

This preparation takes many forms, flowing naturally from a life lived in consciousness of the Divine promise. It manifests in the prayer performed not from habit but from presence, where we truly stand before Allah five times a day, rehearsing for that ultimate standing. It appears in the service we render to others, not for recognition or reciprocation but because we see in every act of kindness an investment in our eternal home. It emerges in the knowledge we seek and share, not for intellectual pride but to draw closer to the One who taught humanity what it knew not.

Perhaps most importantly, this preparation occurs in the quiet moments of character development—the anger swallowed, the forgiveness extended, the patience maintained when every fiber of our being calls for reaction. These invisible victories, witnessed only by Allah, may carry more weight in the eternal scale than any public achievement.

Finding Balance in an Unbalanced World

The promise of the Hereafter shouldn't paralyze us with fear or create a joyless existence focused solely on the afterlife. Instead, it offers a lens through which life gains proper perspective and profound meaning. We can enjoy the permissible pleasures Allah has provided while remembering they're appetizers, not the main course. We can pursue excellence in our worldly endeavors while recognizing that true success is defined by different metrics entirely.

This balance manifests as a unique state of being—engaged but not engrossed, concerned but not consumed, planning but not presuming. We work as if we'll live forever while worshipping as if we'll die tomorrow. We build in this world while investing in the next. We love what Allah has made lawful to love while ensuring that love doesn't compete with our love for Allah and His Messenger.

In our technological age, where distractions multiply exponentially and the temporary feels increasingly permanent through digital preservation, maintaining this balance requires vigilance. Social media creates carefully curated illusions of perfect lives, the news cycle generates perpetual anxiety about worldly matters, and the entertainment industry offers endless escape from spiritual contemplation. Yet these challenges also present opportunities, chances to practice conscious living, to demonstrate that faith can thrive even in the most materialistic of ages.

The Eternal Perspective

When we truly internalize that "Allah's promise is true," every aspect of existence transforms. Difficulties become tests that polish our character for eternal presentation. Blessings become responsibilities that question our gratitude and generosity. Time becomes a precious commodity more valuable than gold, for gold can be earned again but a moment passed is gone forever.

This perspective doesn't diminish our worldly responsibilities—it enhances them. The parent raising children isn't just managing behavior but shepherding souls. The professional at work isn't merely earning a living but establishing a testimony of integrity. The student seeking knowledge isn't just preparing for a career but equipping themselves to better understand and serve their Creator's creation.

Consider how differently we would live if we could see the true nature of our choices—if every act of charity created a palace brick in Paradise, if every moment of sincere remembrance illuminated our graves, if every injustice we patiently endured elevated our eternal station. This isn't fantasy but reality—a reality more real than the screen you're reading these words on, more lasting than the building sheltering you, more certain than tomorrow's sunrise.

A Living Promise

The divine promise isn't merely something to believe in intellectually—it's something to live by practically. It calls us to regular self-assessment, not the kind that produces paralyzing guilt but the kind that generates productive change. It invites us to ask ourselves honest questions: Are my daily choices reflecting eternal priorities or temporary pressures? Am I regularly investing in what lasts or merely maintaining what passes? When I stand in front of Allah, will I wish I had prayed more or scrolled more, served more or accumulated more, forgiven more or held more grudges?

These questions aren't meant to create despair but to inspire action while action is still possible. Every breath brings a new opportunity to prepare for that meeting, every sunrise offers another chance to live with eternal consciousness, every interaction presents a possibility to plant seeds for the eternal harvest.

The promise stands before us—clear, certain, and compelling. The deceptions surround us—subtle, sophisticated, and persistent. The choice remains ours in every moment: Will we allow the temporary to eclipse the eternal? Will we let the Chief Deceiver distort our understanding of the Most Merciful? Or will we live as people who truly believe that Allah's promise is true, navigating this world with our hearts firmly anchored in the next?

In the end, this verse isn't just information to be understood but transformation to be undertaken. It calls us to see through the veils, to live beyond the deceptions, and to prepare for the promise that awaits. For those who heed this call, worldly life becomes not a distraction from the divine but a pathway to it, not a veil over truth but a means to realize it.

Discussion Questions

1. In our technological age, how have the forms of worldly deception evolved while maintaining their essential nature? Consider specific examples from your own experience.
2. How can we maintain consciousness of the Hereafter while fully engaging with our worldly responsibilities? What practical strategies help maintain this balance?
3. Reflect on the concept of trust in Allah's promise. How might deepening this trust transform our response to life's challenges and opportunities?

"O Allah, I ask You for Paradise and whatever words or deeds bring one closer to it, and I seek refuge in You from the Fire and whatever words or deeds bring one closer to it."

22

The Promise of Justice

In the divine wisdom of Islamic teachings, alongside the promises of mercy and reward for the righteous, there stands an equally powerful promise: the absolute certainty of justice and accountability for those who engage in oppression, injustice, and abuse. This promise serves as both a warning and a comfort—warning to those who might be tempted to transgress against others, and comfort to those who suffer under oppression.

The Watchful Eye That Never Closes

Allah's promise regarding accountability for oppression is unequivocal. In Surat Ibrahim, we find a verse that should make every oppressor's heart tremble:

وَلَا تَحْسَبَنَّ ٱللَّهَ غَـٰفِلًا عَمَّا يَعْمَلُ ٱلظَّـٰلِمُونَ ۚ إِنَّمَا يُؤَخِّرُهُمْ لِيَوْمٍ تَشْخَصُ فِيهِ ٱلْأَبْصَـٰرُ

"And never think that Allah is unaware of what the wrongdoers do. He only delays them for a Day when eyes will stare [in horror]." (14:42)

This verse captures the essence of divine justice—that while oppressors may seem to escape worldly consequences, striding through life with apparent impunity, their accountability is merely deferred to a Day when escape will be impossible. The delay is not negligence; it is the rope with which they hang themselves, the time given for either repentance or the accumulation of further evidence against them.

The Prophet ﷺ emphasized the gravity of oppression with a metaphor that haunts the consciousness. He said: "Beware of oppression, for oppression will be darknesses on the Day of Resurrection."[97]

This metaphor of darkness is profound, suggesting not only the spiritual blindness that leads to oppression but also the terrifying consequences that await oppressors—layers upon layers of darkness, each act of oppression adding another veil between them and the light of divine mercy.

The Many Faces of Oppression

Oppression wears countless masks, and divine justice recognizes them all. When it comes to harm, the Qur'an's warning is severe beyond measure:

وَمَن يَقْتُلْ مُؤْمِنًا مُّتَعَمِّدًا فَجَزَآؤُهُۥ جَهَنَّمُ خَٰلِدًا فِيهَا
وَغَضِبَ ٱللَّهُ عَلَيْهِ وَلَعَنَهُۥ وَأَعَدَّ لَهُۥ عَذَابًا عَظِيمًا

"But whoever kills a believer intentionally—his recompense is Hell, wherein he will abide eternally, and Allah has become angry with him and has cursed him and has prepared for him a great punishment." (4:93)

The language here is extraordinary in its severity. Not just punishment, but eternal punishment. Not just divine displeasure, but active divine anger. Not just consequences, but a curse from the Most Merciful. This reflects the sanctity of human life and the magnitude of violating it.

Economic oppression receives equally stern treatment in the divine court. Those who exploit the vulnerable financially are given a visceral warning:

إِنَّ ٱلَّذِينَ يَأْكُلُونَ أَمْوَٰلَ ٱلْيَتَٰمَىٰ ظُلْمًا إِنَّمَا يَأْكُلُونَ فِى بُطُونِهِمْ نَارًا ۖ وَسَيَصْلَوْنَ سَعِيرًا

"Indeed, those who devour the property of orphans unjustly are only consuming into their bellies fire. And they will be burned in a Blaze." (4:10)

The imagery is deliberately graphic; every dirham stolen from the vulnerable, every inheritance denied to the rightful heir, every wage withheld from the worker is transformed into fire that the oppressor consumes, building an inferno within themselves that will manifest fully in the Hereafter.

But oppression isn't limited to physical violence or financial exploitation. The wounds inflicted by the tongue can be equally devastating. The Prophet ﷺ defined a true Muslim as "one from whose tongue and hands other Muslims are safe."[98] This encompasses the spectrum of abuse, such as the parent who destroys a child's self-worth with constant criticism, the spouse who uses words as weapons, and the troll who hides behind anonymity to spread venom.

Lessons Written in History

The Qur'an doesn't merely warn about future accountability; it provides historical evidence of divine justice in action. Pharaoh stands as the archetype of oppression—a man who declared himself divine, who enslaved an entire people, who murdered infants to maintain his power. His end is recorded for all time:

فَأَخَذْنَٰهُ وَجُنُودَهُۥ فَنَبَذْنَٰهُمْ فِى ٱلْيَمِّ ۖ فَٱنظُرْ كَيْفَ كَانَ عَٰقِبَةُ ٱلظَّٰلِمِينَ

"So We seized him and his soldiers, casting them into the sea. See then what was the end of the wrongdoers!" (28:40)

The word "threw" (nabadhnāhum) implies casual disposal, like discarding trash. All of Pharaoh's power, his armies, his monuments, his claimed divinity—thrown into the sea like waste. His preserved body remained a sign for humanity, a reminder that no amount of worldly power can protect from divine justice.

Similarly, the people of ʿĀd represent collective societal oppression. The Qur'an describes them:

فَأَمَّا عَادٌ فَٱسْتَكْبَرُوا۟ فِى ٱلْأَرْضِ بِغَيْرِ ٱلْحَقِّ

"As for ʿĀd, they were arrogant upon the earth without right." (41:15)

Their arrogance manifested in their treatment of the weak, their mockery of divine guidance, their belief that their strength made them invincible. They built monuments to their own glory while crushing those beneath them. Their destruction was so complete that they became nothing more than a cautionary tale, their mighty civilization reduced to ruins covered by sand.

Oppression in Modern Dress

Contemporary forms of oppression may seem more sophisticated, but they fall under the same divine scrutiny. Institutional injustice—where oppression is systematized, bureaucratized, made to seem legitimate through policies and procedures—receives divine attention. Allah warns:

وَلَا تَرْكَنُوٓا۟ إِلَى ٱلَّذِينَ ظَلَمُوا۟ فَتَمَسَّكُمُ ٱلنَّارُ

"And do not incline toward those who do wrong, lest you be touched by the Fire." (11:113)

Even inclining toward oppressors, let alone actively participating in their systems, carries consequences. The bureaucrat who processes unjust evictions, the banker who approves predatory loans, the official who enforces discriminatory policies—all are implicated in the machinery of oppression.

Corporate exploitation represents the modern evolution of economic oppression. Companies that destroy environments for profit, that exploit desperate workers with poverty wages, that deceptively create products designed to fail so consumers must repeatedly purchase—these are contemporary manifestations of ancient forms of injustice.

The digital age has created entirely new avenues for abuse. Cyberbullying can drive victims to despair and even suicide. Online harassment campaigns can destroy reputations and livelihoods. The spreading of private information, the creation of deepfakes and other ill uses of artificial intelligence, the coordination of hate campaigns—all of these fall under the Qur'anic condemnation:

إِنَّ ٱلَّذِينَ يُؤْذُونَ ٱلْمُؤْمِنِينَ وَٱلْمُؤْمِنَـٰتِ بِغَيْرِ مَا ٱكْتَسَبُوا۟ فَقَدِ ٱحْتَمَلُوا۟ بُهْتَـٰنًا وَإِثْمًا مُّبِينًا

"Indeed, those who abuse believing men and believing women undeservedly bear the guilt of slander and manifest sin." (33:58)

The anonymity of the internet provides no cover from the One who sees all, who knows the person behind every username, as the angels record every keystroke typed in hatred.

The Terror of the Final Accounting

The Day of Judgment holds special terror for oppressors because it represents the complete inversion of their worldly experience. Where they once wielded power, they will stand powerless. Where they once hid behind lawyers and lies, every act will be exposed with crystal clarity. Where they once silenced their victims, those victims will speak freely, their testimonies heard and validated.

The Prophet ﷺ described the precision of this accountability with a warning that should make every oppressor seek immediate reconciliation: "Whoever has wronged his brother, let him ask for his pardon before his death, as in the Hereafter there will be neither dinar nor dirham. Before that time, his good deeds will be taken from him and given to his brother, and if he has no good deeds, his brother's sins will be loaded on him."[99]

Imagine the horror of standing on that Day, watching your prayers, your fasting, your charity—all the good deeds you were counting on—being transferred to those you wronged. And when your good deeds run out, watching their sins being loaded onto your scales. Every harsh word, every stolen penny, every moment of abuse literally robbing you of Paradise and dragging you toward Hell.

The confrontation will be direct and unavoidable. No prestigious law firms to hide behind, no public relations teams to manage the narrative, no statute of limitations to invoke. Victims will face their oppressors, and justice will be perfect and complete. The CEO who destroyed countless lives for profits will face every family left destitute. The abusive parent will confront the child whose spirit they crushed. The corrupt official will meet every person whose rights they violated.

The Call to Action

Understanding this promise of accountability should transform how we live. It demands regular self-examination—not the superficial kind that quickly excuses our faults, but deep, honest introspection about how our actions affect others.

Have we used our position to make someone's life harder? Have we withheld what was due to another? Have we stood silent while witnessing oppression?

This promise also calls for immediate rectification of wrongs. The window for seeking forgiveness from those we've wronged closes with death. After that, only the currency of deeds remains, and the exchange rate is devastating for the oppressor. The wise person rushes to make amends while amends are still possible, to return what was taken while return is still an option, to heal wounds while healing can still occur.

Furthermore, this divine promise demands we take an active stance against oppression wherever we encounter it. Silence in the face of injustice is complicity. The Qur'an and Sunnah call us to speak truth to power, to stand with the oppressed, to use whatever means we have—our voices, our resources, our positions—to challenge systems of oppression. This isn't optional; it's a fundamental aspect of faith.

Supporting victims of injustice becomes not just a moral good but a religious obligation. This support takes many forms: believing their accounts, amplifying their voices, providing material assistance, offering emotional support, and working to prevent future victimization. Every act of support for the oppressed is an act of worship, a declaration that we stand on the side of divine justice.

The promise of accountability should also inspire institutional reform efforts. We must work to transform systems that enable oppression, whether in our families, communities, workplaces, or societies. This means challenging unjust policies, creating accountability mechanisms, and building structures that protect the vulnerable rather than exploiting them.

The Door That Remains Open

Despite the severity of these warnings, Islam's message is ultimately one of hope. The door of repentance remains open until the soul reaches the throat, but this forgiveness isn't automatic or unconditional. It requires genuine repentance, which includes recognizing the wrong, feeling remorse, seeking forgiveness from both Allah and those wronged, making restitution where possible, and firmly resolving never to return to that oppression. The one who was once an oppressor can transform into a champion of justice, using their understanding of oppression's mechanisms to dismantle them.

Living Under the Shadow of This Promise

The promise of severe accountability for oppressors serves multiple purposes in Islamic teaching. It deters potential oppression by making clear that no wrongdoing escapes divine notice. It consoles victims with the certainty that their suffering is seen and will be addressed. It maintains hope in ultimate justice when worldly justice fails. And it reminds us all that power, position, and privilege are trusts that we will answer for.

This promise should echo in our minds whenever we're tempted to abuse whatever power we have—whether that's the power of a parent over a child, an employer over an employee, or simply the power of our words to hurt or heal. It should strengthen our resolve when we face oppression, knowing that our oppressor's apparent triumph is temporary and illusory. And it should inspire us to be agents of divine justice in this world, working to establish systems that reflect the perfect justice promised in the next.

The message is clear: every act of oppression is documented, every victim's cry is heard, every wrong will be made right. The only question is whether we'll be standing with the oppressed or the oppressors when that final accounting comes. The choice we make in each moment of moral decision determines not just our earthly legacy but our eternal destination.

Discussion Questions

1. How does the certainty of divine accountability for oppression influence our responsibility to address contemporary forms of institutional injustice?
2. In what ways can we balance the divine promise of severe accountability with the Islamic emphasis on mercy and forgiveness?
3. Consider the psychological impact of believing in ultimate justice. How might this belief affect both oppressors and victims in their worldly interactions?

"O Allah, I seek refuge in You from wronging anyone or being wronged, and I seek refuge in You from going astray or being led astray."

23

The Promise of Safety in the Afterlife

The Day Your Heart Will Sing

My dear reader, in the midst of life's trials and tribulations, there is a promise from Allah that stands as a beacon of hope and reassurance: a promise that on the Day of Judgment, the righteous will find that their journey has been made easy. Imagine a day when every heart trembles, but yours beats with secure peace. A day when terror fills the horizon, but you stand wrapped in divine protection. This is not fantasy; this is Allah's promise to you.

Listen to these words that should be etched in gold upon every believer's heart:

مَن جَآءَ بِٱلْحَسَنَةِ فَلَهُۥ خَيْرٌ مِّنْهَا وَهُم مِّن فَزَعٍ يَوْمَئِذٍ ءَامِنُونَ

"Whoever comes with a good deed will be rewarded with what is better, and they will be secure from the horror on that Day." (27:89)

Do you understand what this means? Every smile you gave when your heart was breaking: multiplied. Every penny you donated when you yourself were struggling: transformed into treasures. Every moment you chose patience over anger, forgiveness over revenge, kindness over indifference, each one becomes a fortress protecting you on the Day when all other fortresses crumble.

Your smallest kindness could become your greatest shield.

When Terror Becomes Tranquility

Picture this: The Day arrives when mountains float like carded wool, when the sky splits apart, when the sun is brought so close that people drown in their own sweat. Humanity stands naked, barefoot, stripped of every pretense, every title, every false dignity. Yet there you stand, clothed in the garments of your good deeds, shaded while others burn, calm while others panic.

This is not because you were perfect. This is because you tried.

Allah captures this transformation in words that should make your soul soar:

إِنَّا نَخَافُ مِن رَّبِّنَا يَوْمًا عَبُوسًا قَمْطَرِيرًا فَوَقَىٰهُمُ ٱللَّهُ شَرَّ ذَٰلِكَ ٱلْيَوْمِ وَلَقَّىٰهُمْ نَضْرَةً وَسُرُورًا

"We fear from our Lord a terribly distressful Day; so Allah will deliver them from the horror of that Day, and grant them radiance and joy." (76:10-11)

Radiance and joy: *naḍrah wa surūr*. Not just safety, not merely protection, but actual radiance emanating from your face, joy flooding your heart. While others wear the darkness of their deeds, you will literally glow with divine light. *The Day everyone else fears will be the day you've been waiting for.*

Think about the teacher who stayed after class to help the struggling student, never knowing that student would grow up to change the world. Think about the mother who woke for *tahajjud* while her children slept, praying for their guidance with tears streaming down her face. Think about the young man who lowered his gaze a thousand times when a thousand temptations called. These are not just good deeds; these are investments in eternity, and the returns are beyond calculation.

The Book That Changes Everything

There comes a moment on that Day, a moment that will define eternity. You will be handed a book. Your book. The complete, unedited story of your life. Every thought, every intention, every secret moment when you chose right over wrong, even when no one was watching.

But here's what the oppressors don't understand: Allah is not looking for a perfect track record but for one that improved; He's looking for sincerity.

The one who receives their book in their right hand, that moment is not just relief, it's vindication. Every time someone mocked your faith, every time you felt alone in your principles, every sacrifice that seemed to go unnoticed, all of it culminates in this single moment when the Creator of the universe publicly acknowledges: "I am pleased with you."

Can you imagine running to your loved ones, book held high, calling out, "Look! Read my record! I made it!" While others try to hide their books behind their backs, while some wish the earth would swallow them, you'll be showing yours to anyone who will look. This is the ultimate twist: the overlooked ones, the ones who were mocked for their faith, they become the kings and queens of that Day.

The Horrors You'll Never Know

There are specific terrors on that Day from which the righteous are protected, and understanding them should make your heart overflow with gratitude.

While wrongdoers experience the crushing weight of regret, that soul-destroying realization of opportunities forever lost, you will feel a satisfaction so complete it defies description. Every moment you spent in prayer while others partied, every temptation you resisted while others indulged, every act of worship performed in the depths of night when only Allah was watching, all of it transforms into an unshakeable contentment. *Regret is the tax on a wasted life, and you won't pay a penny.*

Others will experience the horrific exposure of their secrets, watching their hidden sins played out before all of creation. But for you? Allah will cause your good deeds to become your personal advocate, concealing your faults with divine discretion while amplifying your good deeds until they fill the horizon. That sin you repented from with genuine tears? Erased so thoroughly it's as if it never existed. That good deed you forgot about? Presented to you multiplied seven hundred times over.

The length of standing on that Day will break many: fifty thousand years compressed into a single day of waiting. The sun will be brought within a mile, and people will drown in their own perspiration according to their deeds. But you? You'll be among those shaded under the throne of the Most Merciful, feeling a coolness and comfort that makes those fifty thousand years pass like the time between Ẓuhr and ʿAsr.

And the thirst, the terrible thirst that will plague the guilty, their throats burning with unquenchable fire. But you will drink from al-Kawthar, the Prophet's basin, a drink so pure, so sweet, so perfectly satisfying that you will never experience thirst again. Not on that Day, and not for eternity thereafter. One sip, and you're done with thirst forever.

The Story You're Writing Right Now

My beloved reader, every day you're alive, you're writing your story for that Day. That moment when you restrain your tongue instead of backbiting? That's a sentence in your book. That prayer you perform when you're exhausted? That's a paragraph of light. That parent you serve despite their difficulty, that neighbor you help despite their ingratitude, that money you give despite your own need; these aren't just good deeds, they're your legal defense team for the ultimate court case.

Consider the story of a young man from our time who, despite growing up surrounded by temptation and ease of sin online and offline, chose the path of righteousness. Every Friday, he would visit the elderly in nursing homes, forgotten souls whose own families had completely abandoned them. He would sit with them, listen to their stories, hold their hands. Simple acts, seemingly insignificant in the grand scheme of worldly achievements. But on that Day, each of those forgotten elderly will stand as witnesses for him, and their testimony will carry more weight than any worldly accomplishment. *The forgotten ones you remember will ensure you're never forgotten.*

Our beloved Prophet ﷺ, in his mercy, gave us the secret: The Day of Judgment is terrifying if you've made it terrifying for yourself. For the believer who struggled, who fell and got back up, who sinned and repented, who tried despite failing, that Day is not a fearful consequence for the believers; it's graduation. It's not trial; it's triumph. It's not the end; it's finally, finally, the beginning.

The Choice That Defines Eternity

Here's what could be heart-breaking: Some people reading these words will ignore them. They'll treat Allah's promise like a fairy tale, something to maybe think about when they're older, when life has slowed down, when fun has been had. They don't realize that every passing moment is a withdrawal from a finite account. *You can't deposit time; you can only spend it wisely or waste it permanently.*

But you, dear reader, you who have read this far, you have a choice that others have already forfeited. You can decide, right now, in this moment, that your story will be different. That when that Day arrives, you won't be among those paralyzed by regret, but among those radiant with joy.

It doesn't require perfection. Allah knows you might have shortcomings. But He also gave you the ability to sincerely and permanently repent, to return to Him, to try again. The righteous aren't those who never fall; they're those who never stay down. *Your comeback story is more beloved to Allah than you can imagine.*

The Promise That Changes Everything

Let this truth sink deep into your bones: Every single act of goodness you do is being recorded by angels who never miss a detail. Every prayer in the depths of night, every tear of repentance, every moment of restraint when sin was so easy, all of it is building your case for the Day when all cases are heard.

You know what's beautiful? The same Allah who promises terror for the oppressors promises you peace. The same power that will crush the arrogant will elevate you. The same justice that terrifies the unjust will vindicate you. You're not hoping for mercy from a distant deity; you're counting on a promise from the One who never breaks His word.

The Day of Judgment isn't the day you lose everything; it's the day you finally receive what you've been working for.

May this promise live in your heart like a flame that never dies. May it wake you for Fajr when your bed feels like paradise. May it stop your tongue when gossip would be so delicious. May it open your hand when charity feels difficult. May it lower your gaze when desire pulls strongly. May it soften your heart when anger justifies hardness.

Dear reader, the radiant hope of that secure and joyful Day isn't just waiting for you; it's calling to you, pulling you forward, promising you that every sacrifice is seen, every struggle is recorded, every tear is counted.

Your Day of terror can be your Day of triumph. Your Day of judgment can be your Day of joy. Your Day of exposure can be your Day of elevation.

The choice isn't tomorrow's. The choice is now.

What will you do with it?

Discussion Questions

1. How does the promise of safety on the Day of Judgment influence your daily decisions? Identify one area where this awareness could transform your approach.
2. The chapter mentions that small acts of goodness build cumulative safety. What "small" good deeds could you consistently incorporate into your routine that might have larger spiritual significance?
3. How can we maintain balance between healthy fear of the Day of Judgment and confidence in Allah's promise of safety for the righteous?

O Allah, make us among those who are secure on the Day of the Greatest Terror, and grant us our records in our right hands.

24

The Promise of Paradise

The Garden That Awaits You

Among all of Allah's promises, perhaps none stirs the human heart more profoundly than the promise of Paradise: that eternal abode where every tear becomes joy, every sacrifice finds its reward, and every moment of patient endurance blossoms into everlasting bliss.

وَعَدَ ٱللَّهُ ٱلَّذِينَ ءَامَنُوا۟ وَعَمِلُوا۟ ٱلصَّٰلِحَٰتِ ۙ لَهُم مَّغْفِرَةٌ وَأَجْرٌ عَظِيمٌ

"Allah has promised those who believe and do good 'His' forgiveness and a great reward." (5:9)

Stop for a moment. Let these words sink into your soul. This is not merely an abstract statement written in an ancient book. This is a living, breathing promise from the Creator of the universe to you. Yes, you. The one reading these words right now, perhaps with exhaustion in your eyes from life's struggles, perhaps with a heart heavy from repeated failures, perhaps wondering if your small acts of goodness even matter in this vast universe.

They matter. Every single one matters.

Every act of kindness you've ever done, every sacrifice you've made for the sake of what's right, every humble moment when you chose integrity over easy gain, it's all being recorded by the One who misses nothing. That smile you gave to the lonely cashier when you were having your worst day? Written. That charity you gave when you could barely afford it? Multiplied. That prayer you whispered through your tears when you thought no one was listening? Heard, accepted, and treasured.

The Promise That Cannot Be Broken

وَٱلَّذِينَ ءَامَنُوا۟ وَعَمِلُوا۟ ٱلصَّٰلِحَٰتِ سَنُدْخِلُهُمْ جَنَّٰتٍ تَجْرِى مِن تَحْتِهَا ٱلْأَنْهَٰرُ خَٰلِدِينَ فِيهَآ أَبَدًا ۖ
وَعْدَ ٱللَّهِ حَقًّا ۚ وَمَنْ أَصْدَقُ مِنَ ٱللَّهِ قِيلًا

"And those who believe and do good, We will soon admit them into Gardens under which rivers flow, to stay there for ever and ever. Allah's promise is ˹always˺ true. And whose word is more truthful than Allah's?" (4:122)

Notice how Allah ends this verse with a question that needs no answer: "Whose word is more truthful than Allah's?"

No one's. Absolutely no one's.

Every promise ever broken by someone you trusted, every dream that didn't materialize despite assurances, every time life didn't turn out as promised, all of these disappointments have prepared you to understand the value of this one promise that will never, can never, be broken.

The imagery touches something deep within us: gardens with rivers flowing beneath. For desert dwellers who first heard these words, this was the ultimate luxury. But it's more than physical description. It's the promise of flow after stagnation, of life after death, of abundance after scarcity. Those rivers that flow beneath Paradise? They're washing away every moment of thirst you endured, every tear you shed, every time you felt dried up inside but kept going anyway.

Beyond Your Wildest Dreams

Perhaps the most breathtaking aspect of Paradise is that it exceeds the boundaries of human imagination. The Prophet ﷺ conveyed a hadith qudsi where Allah says: "I have prepared for My righteous servants what no eye has seen, no ear has heard, and no human heart has ever conceived."[100]

Close your eyes and think of the most beautiful thing you've ever seen. That sunset that made you forget to breathe. That newborn's face that made you believe in miracles. That view from the mountain that made you whisper "SubḥānAllāh" without thinking.

Paradise is infinitely more beautiful.

Think of the most melodious sound you've ever heard. Your mother's lullaby when you were scared. The call to prayer that made you weep.

Paradise's sounds are infinitely sweeter.

Think of the greatest joy your heart has ever felt. The moment you held your child. The day you were forgiven by someone you'd wronged. The second you realized Allah had answered your impossible du'aa.

Paradise's joy is infinitely greater.

This isn't exaggeration. This is Allah telling you that your human mind, as magnificent as it is, cannot even begin to imagine what He has prepared for you. Every limitation you've ever felt, every boundary that's constrained you, every ceiling you've hit, Paradise shatters them all.

Your Eternal Home

جَنَّٰتِ عَدْنٍ ٱلَّتِى وَعَدَ ٱلرَّحْمَٰنُ عِبَادَهُۥ بِٱلْغَيْبِ ۚ إِنَّهُۥ كَانَ وَعْدُهُۥ مَأْتِيًّا

"⌜They will be in⌝ the Gardens of Eternity, promised in trust by the Most Compassionate to His servants. Surely His promise will be fulfilled." (19:61)

The Arabic word "ʿadn" means permanence, establishment, settledness. Do you know what this means for you, you who've moved so many times, you who've never felt truly secure, you who've always worried about tomorrow?

It means you're going home. Really home. Forever home.

No more rent increases. No more eviction notices. No more looking over your shoulder. No more anxiety about where you'll be next year. Paradise is the home where you'll finally unpack completely, knowing you'll never have to pack again.

Sister Khadija lost her home three times to war. Three times she watched everything she'd built disappear in smoke and rubble. But she told her children through tears that became smiles: "We're not working for a home here. We're working for a home that no bomb can destroy, no army can steal, no government can seize. Every box we pack, every mile we walk as refugees, we're walking toward our real home."

Your struggles are not meaningless wandering. They're the journey home.

The Greatest Gift of All

While Paradise offers unimaginable physical delights, the Qur'an reveals something that should make your heart race:

وَعَدَ ٱللَّهُ ٱلْمُؤْمِنِينَ وَٱلْمُؤْمِنَٰتِ جَنَّٰتٍ تَجْرِى مِن تَحْتِهَا ٱلْأَنْهَٰرُ خَٰلِدِينَ فِيهَا وَمَسَٰكِنَ طَيِّبَةً فِى
جَنَّٰتِ عَدْنٍ ۚ وَرِضْوَٰنٌ مِّنَ ٱللَّهِ أَكْبَرُ ۚ ذَٰلِكَ هُوَ ٱلْفَوْزُ ٱلْعَظِيمُ

"Allah has promised the believers, both men and women, Gardens under which rivers flow, to stay there forever, and splendid homes in the Gardens of Eternity, and, above all, the pleasure of Allah. That is truly the ultimate triumph." (9:72)

"The pleasure of Allah is greater." Greater than eternal gardens. Greater than perfect homes. Greater than every pleasure combined.

Do you understand what this means? The Creator of a hundred billion galaxies, the Designer of DNA, the Author of love itself, will be pleased with you. Not tolerant. Not accepting. Pleased.

Every night you stayed up wondering if you were enough, every day you felt like a failure, every moment you thought your efforts were worthless, all of it will evaporate in the moment you realize that Allah, the Most High, is pleased with you.

Sheikh Abdullah spent forty years teaching Qur'an in a small village mosque. No fame, no fortune, just decades of patient teaching. He once said: "I've met billionaires who can't sleep, tormented by whether their lives have meaning. But I sleep peacefully knowing that if I reach Paradise, I'll have achieved something no amount of money can buy: the pleasure of the One who created money itself."

When Every Tear Makes Sense

One of Paradise's most beautiful moments is captured in this verse:

وَقَالُوا۟ ٱلْحَمْدُ لِلَّهِ ٱلَّذِى صَدَقَنَا وَعْدَهُۥ وَأَوْرَثَنَا ٱلْأَرْضَ نَتَبَوَّأُ

مِنَ ٱلْجَنَّةِ حَيْثُ نَشَآءُ ۖ فَنِعْمَ أَجْرُ ٱلْعَـٰمِلِينَ

"They will say, 'Praise be to Allah Who has fulfilled His promise to us, and made us inherit this land to settle in Paradise wherever we please. How excellent is the reward of those who work righteousness!'" (39:74)

Imagine that moment. You're standing in Paradise, looking back at your life, and suddenly every single thing makes sense. That heartbreak that devastated you? It was redirecting you to your destiny. That job you lost? It was freeing you for better worship. That illness that broke your body? It was purifying your soul for this moment.

And you'll say, with tears of joy streaming down your face, "He kept His promise. Allah kept His promise to me."

Every struggle was a blessing in disguise. Every test was a gift wrapped in difficulty.

The Stories That Give Us Hope

Ahmed was a teacher in rural Morocco. For thirty years, he educated village children while earning barely enough to survive. Multiple times, schools in the city offered him positions with ten times the salary. He refused every time, saying, "These children need me more than I need money."

His colleagues thought he was foolish. His own brothers called him stubborn. But Ahmed would smile and quote the hadith: "The world is a prison for the believer and paradise for the disbeliever." This wasn't pessimism; this was perspective. Every moment of sacrifice was building his eternal mansion.

When Ahmed died, hundreds of his former students came to his funeral. Doctors, engineers, teachers, all crying for the man who had chosen them over comfort. If his earthly impact was this profound, can you imagine his heavenly reward? Can you imagine his joy when he sees that every equation he taught, every letter he helped a child write, every moment of patience with difficult students, all of it transformed into eternal treasures?

Your sacrifices aren't disappearing into nothing. They're being transformed into forever.

Or consider Maryam, the nurse who worked in war zones. She could have had a comfortable position in any private hospital. Instead, she chose to treat victims of violence, often working without proper supplies, sometimes without pay, always without safety.

When asked why, she said something that should be written in gold: "Every person I help could be my ticket to Paradise. Allah says that saving one life is like saving all humanity. So, every day, I might be saving all humanity."

Her colleague found her crying after losing a child patient to a bombing. Through her tears, she whispered, "This innocent soul is already in Paradise. My test is whether I'll join them there." She turned tragedy into hope, loss into motivation, grief into determination.

Your pain is not punishment. It's preparation for a joy you can't yet imagine.

The Confirmation of Truth

Allah ﷻ gives us a glimpse of a profound moment:

وَنَادَىٰٓ أَصْحَـٰبُ ٱلْجَنَّةِ أَصْحَـٰبَ ٱلنَّارِ أَن قَدْ وَجَدْنَا مَا وَعَدَنَا
رَبُّنَا حَقًّا فَهَلْ وَجَدتُّم مَّا وَعَدَ رَبُّكُمْ حَقًّا

"The residents of Paradise will call out to the residents of the Fire, 'We have certainly found our Lord's promise to be true. Have you too found your Lord's promise to be true?'" (7:44)

This isn't gloating. This is the final vindication of every moment you were mocked for your faith, every time you were called backward for your beliefs, every instance where you or others wondered if you were wasting your life on something that might not be real. It was real. It was all real. More real than anything else.

The Path That's Crystal Clear

The beautiful thing about Paradise is that the path to it isn't hidden or mysterious. Allah hasn't made it a secret available only to the elite. The path is illuminated, marked, and accessible to everyone:

Faith (īmān) that lives in your heart and changes how you see everything. Not blind faith, but faith with eyes wide open to Allah's signs everywhere.

Righteous action ('amal ṣāliḥ) that flows naturally from that faith. Not perfection, but consistent effort. Not sinlessness, but sincere striving.

Sincerity (ikhlāṣ) that purifies everything you do. Not for social media likes, not for people's praise, but for the One whose opinion actually matters eternally.

Perseverance (ṣabr) that keeps you going when everyone else quits. Not because you're strong, but because you know Who you're living for.

Repentance (tawbah) that washes you clean again and again. Not because you're worthless, but because you're worth purifying.

The Mercy That Changes Everything

Here's the secret that should make you weep with relief. The Prophet ﷺ said: "None of you will enter Paradise by virtue of his deeds alone." They asked, "Not even you, O Messenger of Allah?" He said, "Not even me, unless Allah covers me with His mercy."[101]

Do you understand the liberation in these words? Paradise isn't a wage you earn; it's a gift you receive. You don't have to be perfect. You don't have to never fall. You just have to keep trying, keep turning back, keep reaching for His mercy that's always, always reaching for you.

Ruqayyah from Ireland struggled her whole life with feeling "never good enough." Every prayer felt inadequate, every good deed felt too small. Then she understood this hadith, and it transformed her entire relationship with Allah. She said: "I stopped seeing Paradise as an exam I might fail and started seeing it as a gift Allah wants to give me. My worship changed from fearful performance to grateful conversation."

Paradise isn't a prize for the perfect. It's a gift for the grateful.

Living with Paradise in Your Heart

This promise of Paradise isn't meant to make you passive about earthly life. It's meant to set your soul on fire with purpose. When you know that every smile counts, every kindness matters, every moment of patience is building your eternal home, suddenly nothing is mundane anymore.

The exhausted parent realizes that every sleepless night with a crying baby is witnessed and rewarded by the One who never sleeps. The employee who maintains integrity while everyone else cheats knows that each ethical choice is a brick in their palace. The student struggling through difficult studies understands that beneficial knowledge becomes a flowing river of reward that never stops.

Every moment of your life can be an investment in eternity.

The Ultimate Triumph

Allah calls Paradise "the ultimate triumph" (*al-fawz al-ʿaẓīm*). Not *a* triumph. Not *great* triumph. The *ultimate* triumph.

Every other success story ends. The wealthy die and leave their wealth. The famous are forgotten. The powerful become powerless. But Paradise? Paradise is success that never ends, joy that never fades, achievement that actually lasts.

As you read these words, perhaps your heart is stirring with something you haven't felt in a long time: hope. Real hope. Not the fragile hope in worldly outcomes that might disappoint, but hope in a promise from the One who never disappoints.

Your tears matter. Your struggles count. Your efforts are seen. Your pain has purpose. Your life has meaning that transcends this moment, this day, this entire earthly existence.

When this world weighs heavy on your shoulders, when injustice seems to win, when being good feels pointless, when everyone else seems to prosper through evil while you suffer for righteousness, remember: You're not living for these fleeting moments. You're investing in an eternal reality where every tear becomes a pearl, every sacrifice becomes a treasure, and every moment of faith becomes an everlasting joy.

This is Allah's promise to you. More certain than tomorrow's sunrise, more real than the ground beneath your feet, more valuable than everything this world could ever offer.

The question isn't whether Paradise exists. The question isn't whether you can reach it. The question is: Will you let this promise transform how you live today?

Will you smile at that difficult person, knowing it's building your garden? Will you give that charity, knowing it's furnishing your eternal home? Will you make that prayer, knowing it's your conversation with the One who's preparing your place? Will you choose righteousness, even when it costs you, knowing the payment waiting for you is beyond calculation?

Paradise isn't just waiting for you. It's calling to you, pulling you forward, cheering you on.

Every prophet faced rejection but kept preaching because they knew about Paradise. Every martyr faced death with a smile because they knew about Paradise. Every mother who sacrificed everything for her children did so because she knew about Paradise. Every righteous person who chose the difficult right over the easy wrong did so because they knew about Paradise.

Now you know too.

May Allah grant us the faith to believe in His promise, the strength to work toward it, and the mercy to receive it. May we be among those who will declare with joy: "Praise be to Allah Who has fulfilled His promise to us!"

May we meet in gardens beneath which rivers flow, where every tear is forgotten, every pain is healed, and every dream we ever had about happiness is exceeded beyond our wildest imagination.

Discussion Questions

1. How does the promise of Paradise, particularly the aspect that it exceeds human imagination, influence your daily decisions and help you through difficulties?
2. The chapter mentions that Paradise is ultimately Allah's mercy rather than something earned. How does this understanding affect your approach to worship and good deeds?
3. In what practical ways can we maintain consciousness of Paradise without becoming disconnected from our earthly responsibilities and relationships?

"O Allah, we ask You for Paradise and whatever words and deeds bring us closer to it."

25

The Promise of Eternal Reunion

The Promise That Heals Every Goodbye

There exists no pain quite like separation from those we love. Whether through death, distance, or circumstance, the ache of missing beloved faces and voices touches the deepest parts of our souls. Yet Allah, in His infinite mercy and understanding of the human heart, has given us a promise that transforms every temporary goodbye into a prelude to eternal reunion.

وَٱلَّذِينَ ءَامَنُوا۟ وَٱتَّبَعَتْهُمْ ذُرِّيَّتُهُم بِإِيمَـٰنٍ أَلْحَقْنَا بِهِمْ ذُرِّيَّتَهُمْ
وَمَآ أَلَتْنَـٰهُم مِّنْ عَمَلِهِم مِّن شَىْءٍ ۚ كُلُّ ٱمْرِئٍۭ بِمَا كَسَبَ رَهِينٌ

"As for those who believe and whose descendants follow them in faith, We will elevate their descendants to their rank, never discounting anything of the reward of their deeds. Every person will reap only what they sowed." (52:21)

Read that again. Let it sink deep into your grieving heart. Allah doesn't merely promise that righteous families might meet occasionally in Paradise. The Arabic word "alḥaqna" means to join permanently, to unite inseparably. Your family in Paradise won't be visitors you occasionally see; they'll be your eternal companions in joy.

Every goodbye you've ever said was actually "see you later."

When Death Feels Like the End

Bassam stood at his mother's grave, the fresh earth still dark with morning dew. She had passed away just three days ago, and the wound felt too raw to bear. As the cemetery keeper approached to close the gates, Bassam found himself unable to leave.

"She was everything to me," he told the old man. "She raised five of us alone after my father died. Never complained, never showed us her struggles. Just loved us with everything she had. How do I go on knowing I'll never hear her voice again?"

The cemetery keeper, who had witnessed countless grieving souls, sat beside him on the cold stone bench. "Young man, do you remember what the Prophet ﷺ said about our parents in Paradise?"

When Bassam stayed quiet, the keeper continued, "He said that Allah will elevate the rank of righteous servants in Paradise, and when they ask how they earned such elevation, Allah will tell them it was through their children's prayers for them."

The keeper paused, letting the words settle. "Your mother's story with you isn't ending here; it's transforming. Every prayer you make for her forgiveness, every charity you give in her name, every good deed you do thinking of her teachings, all of it reaches her."

Bassam's tears didn't stop, but something shifted in his heart. His grief remained, but alongside it grew a different emotion: anticipation. His relationship with his mother hadn't ended; it had entered a new phase. He could still serve her, still honor her, still contribute to her eternal happiness through his prayers and deeds.

Death is not a wall between you and your loved ones. It's just a veil, and veils can be pierced by prayer.

This understanding revolutionizes how we process loss. The Prophet ﷺ taught us that when we pray for our deceased parents, angels carry these prayers to them like gifts, bringing them joy in their graves and elevation in their ranks. Your mother who passed ten years ago? She knows when you make du'aa for her. Your father whose approval you always sought? He receives your prayers like bouquets of light.

The Woman Who Lost Everyone

The elderly woman sat by the window of her empty apartment, photographs spread across her lap. Each image captured a moment frozen in time: her husband's gentle smile, her children's laughter, grandchildren she'd never met in person. Umm Abdullah had lost seventeen family members in the genocide. Seventeen souls who once filled her life with warmth and purpose.

Her neighbor found her there one evening, tears tracing familiar paths down her weathered cheeks. "Habibti, you're crying again," the young woman said gently.

Umm Abdullah looked up, and to her neighbor's surprise, she was smiling through her tears. "These aren't tears of despair, habibti. I was remembering what my husband told me before he died. He said, 'Don't grieve too long, my love. This separation is just a blink. We have eternity waiting for us.'"

She picked up a worn Qur'an from the table, its pages soft from years of turning, and opened it to a verse marked with a faded ribbon. Her voice, though aged, carried unwavering certainty:

"You see," Umm Abdullah continued, her eyes bright with a hope that defied her circumstances, "Allah doesn't just promise Paradise. He promises we'll be together there. My children, my grandchildren, my beloved husband, we're not lost to each other. We're just waiting in different rooms until the door opens to bring us together forever."

She traced the faces in the photographs with trembling fingers. "Sometimes I imagine the reunion. My husband will look young again, that smile that captured my heart sixty years ago. My children will run to me like they did when they were small. My mother, who I haven't seen in forty years, will hold me again. And this time, there will be no more goodbyes. Not ever."

Your loved ones aren't gone. They're just waiting for you on the other side of temporary.

When Children Go First

Sometimes the natural order seems reversed, and children precede their parents to the next life. This particular pain, a parent burying their child, is considered among the most difficult trials humans can face. Yet even here, especially here, Allah's promise brings extraordinary comfort.

The Prophet ﷺ said that children who die before reaching the age of accountability are in Paradise, and he witnessed them in a true dream under the care of Prophet Ibrahim ﷺ, playing freely and joyfully until the Day of Judgment.[102] But here's what breaks and then mends the heart: these children will take their parents by the hand and refuse to let go until Allah admits them all to Paradise together.

Your child whom you thought you lost becomes your guide to eternal bliss.

Fatima lost her eight-year-old daughter Nusayba to leukemia. For months, she couldn't enter Nusayba's room without collapsing in grief. The small pink backpack still hanging on the door hook, the half-finished drawing on the desk, the teddy bear that still smelled like her daughter, everything was a dagger to her heart.

Then one night, she dreamed of Nusayba in a garden more beautiful than anything she'd ever imagined. Her daughter was laughing, surrounded by other children, her hair flowing in a breeze that seemed to carry the scent of Paradise itself. When Nusayba saw her mother in the dream, she ran to her with joy.

"Mama, don't cry for me," dream-Nusayba said, her hands cupping her mother's face. "I'm keeping your place ready here. We have the most beautiful house waiting for us, and I water the gardens every day so they'll be perfect when you come."

When Nusayba woke, her pillow was soaked with tears, but they were different tears. The crushing weight on her chest had lifted slightly. The dream might have been just her subconscious, but it aligned perfectly with what the Prophet ﷺ taught about children in Paradise. Her daughter hadn't ceased to exist; she had simply gone ahead to prepare their eternal home.

Now, when Fatima enters Nusayba's room, she doesn't just see absence. She sees a child who is waiting, preparing, perhaps even praying for her mother to join her in gardens where no illness exists, where no separation occurs, where every day is joy without end.

Building Paradise Together Now

The promise of family reunion in Paradise isn't passive; it's something we actively build through our choices and actions. Every moment you spend teaching your child about Allah, every family gathering where you remember Him together, every act of patience with difficult relatives for the sake of Allah, all of these are constructing your eternal home together.

Ahmad, a father of four, transformed his understanding of parenting when he truly grasped this promise. "I used to focus so much on my kids' worldly success: their grades, their careers, their financial security. I would lose sleep over their test scores and university applications."

His voice breaks as he continues, "But when I understood that we could be together forever in Paradise, my priorities changed. Now when I wake them for Fajr, even when they groan and complain, I think: 'I'm not just waking them for prayer. I'm securing our eternity together.' When I teach them Qur'an, even when they'd rather play video games, I remember: 'These verses will unite us forever.'"

He pulls out his phone to show a family photo. "I'm not just raising them for eighty years in this world. I'm trying to secure our forever. Every bedtime story about the prophets, every moment I bite my tongue instead of yelling, every time I choose patience over anger, I'm building our eternal home."

Every act of love toward your family is a brick in your palace in Paradise.

Consider the beautiful thought that when a person enters Paradise, they will ask about their parents, spouses, and children. If any of them are missing due to lower ranks, the person will intercede for them, and Allah, in His mercy, will elevate them to be together.

Think about what this means. Your righteous grandmother who always prayed for you? She's waiting to pull you up to her level. Your child whom you raised with such patience and love? They'll refuse to enter their palace without you. The bonds of family, when rooted in faith, become eternal elevators, each member pulling the others toward higher ranks of Paradise.

When Your Family Doesn't Believe

Not everyone comes from righteous families. Some reading this might be thinking, "This promise doesn't apply to me. My family doesn't believe, or they've hurt me, or we're estranged." Your heart might be breaking not from loss but from the fear of eternal separation from those you love despite their flaws.

But here's where Allah's mercy expands even further.

First, remember that you could be the one who brings faith to your family line. You could be the ancestor future generations pray for, the one who changed the family's eternal trajectory. The Prophet ﷺ had a few ancestors who were idol worshippers, yet he became the seal of the prophets. Some of his own family members rejected Islam despite the overwhelming evidence, while the majority embraced it.

A brother in Norway converted to Islam despite his family's opposition. For years, he grieved the potential loss of his birth family in the afterlife. "I would cry in sujood, begging Allah to guide them. The thought of Paradise without my mother, who sacrificed everything for me, felt like it wouldn't be Paradise at all."

But then he realized something profound: "Every person who taught me to pray, every brother who supported me when my family rejected me, every friend who invited me for Eid when I had nowhere to go, they all became my family for eternity. Paradise isn't about losing family; it's about gaining a family as vast as the entire ummah of believers."

Furthermore, your prayers for your non-Muslim family matter. While alive, your example and prayers might be what guides them. Never stop praying for them. Your persistent du'aa might be the key that eventually opens their hearts.

Sometimes the family you're born into is just the starting point. The family you build through faith becomes your eternal tribe.

Glimpses of Forever

There are moments in this world that give us glimpses of our promised reunion in Paradise. When families or friends gather to break fast together in Ramadan, when multiple generations stand side by side in prayer, when elderly parents are surrounded by children and grandchildren who still seek their blessings, these moments are rehearsals for eternity.

Umm Hassan, a grandmother of twelve, makes her home the center of family gatherings every Friday. Her small apartment somehow fits everyone, with grandchildren sitting on the floor, adult children squeezed on couches, and the newest babies passed from arm to arm.

"People ask me why I insist on these weekly gatherings when everyone is so busy," she says, her eyes twinkling. "I tell them that we're practicing for Paradise. Every

Friday when I see four generations of my family praying together, laughing together, sharing meals together, I see a preview of our eternal life."

She pauses to help her youngest grandchild with his food. "You see this controlled chaos? This beautiful noise of family? In Paradise, it will be like this but perfect. No one will have to leave early for work. No one will get tired. No one will argue about anything. Just pure love, forever and ever."

The most beautiful aspect of these earthly gatherings is how they pale in comparison to what awaits. If the joy of seeing your loved ones for a few hours each week fills your heart, imagine the joy of eternal togetherness with no goodbyes, no conflicts, no misunderstandings, just pure love and happiness that never ends.

Love Letters to Heaven

When Sameer's wife of forty years passed away, his children worried about him living alone. They expected to find him destroyed, perhaps unable to function. Instead, while he missed her deeply, he carried himself with remarkable peace.

"Every night before I sleep," he explained to his concerned daughter, "I make du'aa for her. I think about how our grandson looks just like her, about how I finally fixed that squeaky door she always complained about. I imagine myself telling her to be patient and that I'm coming soon."

His eyes, though wet with tears, shine with certainty. "This separation is temporary. We had forty years here; we'll have forever there. When I think of it that way, these remaining years feel like minutes." He shows his daughter a notebook where he writes letters to his wife. "I write what I would tell her if she were here. One day, in Paradise, I'll tell her everything in person God-willing. And she'll tell me about her journey too. We'll have literally forever to catch up."

Grief is just love with nowhere to go in this world. In Paradise, that love finds its home again.

Preparing for the Ultimate Reunion

The promise of eternal family reunion calls us to action in beautiful ways. It means seeing every family member not just as a temporary companion but as a potential eternal friend. It transforms how we handle family conflicts: is any disagreement worth risking eternal separation? It revolutionizes our priorities: what good is leaving our children wealth if we don't secure their eternal inheritance?

Start today. Make that phone call to the relative you've been avoiding. Say "I love you" to your teenager who acts like they don't care. Forgive that family member who hurt you; the wound they caused is temporary, but unforgiveness could separate you forever. Teach your children another verse of Qur'an; each verse is a rope binding you together for eternity. Pray for your parents, living or deceased; your prayers are gifts that reach them wherever they are.

Every one of these actions is building toward the moment when you'll stand together in Paradise, looking back at the journey with gratitude for every step that brought you there.

The Moment of Reunion

Close your eyes and imagine it, really imagine it. You've just entered Paradise, still in awe of its beauty, when you hear a voice calling your name. Not just any voice, but *the* voice, the one you've missed, the one you thought you'd never hear again.

You turn, and there they are. Your mother, looking exactly as she did in her best years, but more radiant. Your father, with that smile you inherited. Your grandparents you barely remember from childhood. Your spouse who left too soon. Your child who went ahead to prepare your place.

But they're not as they were, pained by illness, aged by time, burdened by worry. They're perfected, radiating light, their faces glowing with a joy that has no shadow. And when they embrace you, it's not the careful, time-limited embraces of Earth. It's the embrace of eternity, where no one ever has to let go again.

Your mother doesn't have to worry about bills anymore. Your father doesn't carry the weight of providing. Your child doesn't know fear or pain. Your spouse doesn't have the insecurities that sometimes created distance. Every dysfunction that plagued your earthly family is gone. Every hurt is healed. Every relationship is exactly as it should have been all along.

And the conversation! Oh, the conversations you'll have. "Tell me about your journey after I left," imagine them saying. And you'll have forever to tell them. No rushing because visiting hours are ending. No holding back because time is limited. Just endless, perfect communion with the souls you love most.

In Paradise, every family becomes the family they were always meant to be.

The Promise That Keeps Us Going

As we navigate this temporary life with all its separations and challenges, let this promise be the light that guides us home. When your baby keeps you up all night, remember you're not just soothing a crying infant; you're building a relationship that will last forever. When caring for your parent becomes overwhelming, remember you're serving someone who might pull you into Paradise. When your teenager tests your patience, remember that your gentle response might be what keeps them in faith and secures your eternity together.

Umm Abdullah, whom we met at the beginning, now runs a support group for war widows and mothers who've lost children. She tells them all the same thing:

"We're not just grieving. We're waiting. And while we wait, we prepare. Every prayer, every good deed, every act of patience, it's all preparation for the greatest family reunion ever promised."

She holds up her photographs. "These faces? They're not memories. They're appointments. I have an appointment with each of them, and I will not miss it."

This is Allah's promise to those who believe and whose families follow them in faith: not just Paradise, but Paradise together. Not just eternal life, but eternal life with those we love most. Not just peace, but shared peace with the souls that matter most to our hearts.

The question isn't whether this reunion will happen; Allah's promises are always fulfilled. The question is whether we're preparing ourselves and our families to be part of it. Every day we have with our families is an opportunity to strengthen the faith that will unite us forever. Every prayer we teach our children, every moment of patience with difficult relatives, every act of forgiveness within our families, all of it is building toward the eternal reunion that no force can ever break.

Death cannot separate what faith has joined together.

Every goodbye in this world is just a temporary pause in an eternal conversation.

Your family story doesn't end at the grave. That's just the chapter break before "happily ever after."

Tonight, before you sleep, remember the faces of those you love, or hold the memory of those who've gone ahead. Imagine telling them, in your heart: "I'll see you in Paradise. Wait for me. I'm coming. We'll be together forever." This thought is for you, for your own motivation and perseverance. And then live tomorrow like someone preparing for the greatest reunion ever promised.

Discussion Questions

1. How does the promise of eternal family reunion change your perspective on current family challenges and the effort required to maintain family bonds?
2. For those who have lost loved ones, how might this promise transform grief from despair into hopeful anticipation? What practical steps can maintain connection with deceased family members through prayer and good deeds?
3. Given that Paradise extends the concept of family beyond blood relations to include all believers, how might this expand our understanding of spiritual family and community?

"Our Lord, grant us from among our spouses and offspring comfort to our eyes and make us an example for the righteous."

26

The Promise of Seeing Allah

Among the most profound promises of the afterlife stands one that surpasses all others in its magnificence—the promise that the believers will see their Lord in Paradise. This divine assurance represents the pinnacle of human aspiration and the ultimate fulfillment of our spiritual journey. It is a promise that transforms our understanding of Paradise from a place of mere physical pleasure to one of supreme spiritual completion.

With characteristic eloquence, the Qur'an speaks of this momentous event:

وُجُوهٌ يَوْمَئِذٍ نَّاضِرَةٌ

إِلَىٰ رَبِّهَا نَاظِرَةٌ

"On that Day [some] faces will be radiant and bright,
looking at their Lord." (75: 22-23)

The Arabic word "*nādhirah*" (radiant) suggests a luminosity born of joy and anticipation, while "*nādhirah*" (looking) implies direct vision. This verse captures not just the act of seeing but the state of those blessed with this vision, their faces gleaming with the light of divine proximity.

The Prophet ﷺ provided a beautiful clarification of this promise through an analogy that resonates with human experience. When asked about seeing Allah ﷻ on the Day of Resurrection, he drew a comparison with the most visible celestial bodies known to humanity. The exchange, preserved in authentic traditions, unfolds with remarkable clarity: "You will see your Lord as you see this full moon, and you will have no trouble in seeing Him."[103]

These reports about the ultimate reward of paradise, reported by many companions, establishes not just the reality of seeing Allah but its clarity and certainty. The many hadith analogies with the sun and moon, objects whose visibility is unmistakable, emphasizes that this vision will be real, direct, and free from any ambiguity.

The Journey to Divine Vision

The path to this supreme moment traverses remarkable stations. Beginning with the departure from earthly life, passing through the grave, and proceeding through the momentous events of the Day of Judgment, the believer encounters increasingly profound manifestations of divine power and mercy.

They witness the angels, experience the reckoning (ḥisāb), cross the bridge (ṣirāṭ), and finally enter Paradise. Each stage prepares the soul for what lies beyond, the ultimate honor of beholding the Creator of everything.

The Day of More (Yawm al-Mazīd)

A particularly moving hadith describes a special gathering in Paradise known as Yawm al-Mazīd. The Prophet ﷺ related that Jibrīl explained this as a weekly gathering where Allah ﷻ grants His creation even more than the countless pleasures of Paradise. The scene described is one of unprecedented honor:

The Lord descends from His Throne to His Kursī, while seats of light accommodate the Prophets and golden footstools seat the martyrs. The rest of Paradise's inhabitants sit upon hills of musk, yet all feel equally honored in this divine presence. Then comes the moment of ultimate generosity—Allah asks them to express their desires, and they unanimously request His pleasure. He grants them this and more, bestowing upon them "that which no eye has seen, no ear has heard, and it has not crossed the mind of any human."[104]

The Unveiling

This culminating moment is captured in another profound hadith where Allah ﷻ asks the people of Paradise if they desire anything more. After acknowledging His previous favors, the brightening of their faces, admission to Paradise, salvation from Hell, the ultimate veil is lifted. The prophet ﷺ tells us that "they will not have been given anything more dear to them than looking upon their Lord."[105] This is what Allah refers to in the verse:

لِّلَّذِينَ أَحْسَنُوا۟ ٱلْحُسْنَىٰ وَزِيَادَةٌ

"Those who do good will have the finest reward and [even] more." (10:26)

The "more" (ziyādah) mentioned here has been clarified by the prophet ﷺ as this supreme gift of seeing Allah. Understanding this promise transforms our earthly journey. As one scholar beautifully noted, "Every step you take in this world either brings you closer to seeing Allah or being prevented from seeing Him." This reality fills our daily choices with profound significance. The merchandise of Allah, as the Prophet ﷺ reminded us, is expensive: "Indeed, the merchandise of Allah is expensive; indeed, the merchandise of Allah is Paradise."

One of the most merciful aspects of this promise is that in Paradise, negative emotions cannot touch its inhabitants. Were it possible to feel shame or unworthiness in Paradise, the overwhelming honor of beholding Allah might bring even the most righteous to tears of regret over their worldly shortcomings. Yet Allah's mercy removes all such feelings, allowing the believers to experience this supreme gift with pure joy and gratitude.

Imagine the profound moment when Allah calls out: "O people of Paradise, where are my servants who worshiped me without ever seeing me?" This call honors those who maintained faith despite never witnessing their Lord, who persevered in worship while relying solely on inner conviction. Their reward becomes all the more sweet for their patience and steadfastness in faith.

Contemporary Relevance

In our modern world, where instant gratification often overshadows long-term aspirations, this promise reminds us that our ultimate fulfillment lies not in temporary pleasures but in the eternal joy of divine proximity. For those facing hardship, oppression, or doubt, it offers the assurance that every difficulty endured for Allah's sake brings them closer to this supreme moment.

The Value of Preparation

The Prophet ﷺ taught that "Whoever fears (Allah) sets out at nightfall, and whoever sets out at nightfall will reach their goal."[106] This metaphor of night travel suggests that preparation for this ultimate meeting requires sacrifice and vigilance. Just as travelers in ancient times would set out at night to avoid the desert heat, believers must sometimes forsake immediate comforts for the greater goal. Some scholars believed this hadith to also refer to the night prayer, and for the believer to generally be wary of the traps of the devil throughout life.

Personal Reflection

When we contemplate what it might mean to behold Allah, human language falls short. Attempts to imagine this moment serve not to capture its reality but to inspire preparation for it. The proper response might well be speechless awe, as words cannot encompass the majesty of such an encounter.

Consider the prophets and messengers, who experienced various manifestations of divine power in this world—how will they respond to this direct vision? Think of the believers who were oppressed and persecuted, yet maintained their faith, how will their patience be rewarded with this supreme honor?

The hadith reminding us that "the merchandise of Allah is expensive" takes on new meaning in light of this promise. Whatever sacrifices we make in this life pale in comparison to this reward. Every good deed that continues to benefit others after our death, every act of charity that strains our resources, every moment of patience in adversity becomes an investment in this ultimate goal.

A Promise That Transforms

Understanding this promise should transform our daily lives in several ways:

First, it should instill a sense of purpose and direction in our worship. Every prayer becomes not just a ritual but a step toward this supreme meeting. Every act of charity, every moment of patience, every struggle against our lower desires becomes preparation for this ultimate honor.

Second, it should affect how we view worldly trials and tribulations. When we truly internalize that every difficulty endured for Allah's sake brings us closer to beholding Him, hardships become more bearable, even welcome as means of purification and elevation.

Finally, it should influence our interactions with creation. Knowing that our treatment of others and our conduct in this world either qualify or disqualify us for this supreme honor should make us more mindful of our behavior and more conscious of our responsibilities.

Conclusion

The promise of seeing Allah ﷻ represents the pinnacle of Paradise's pleasures and the ultimate fulfillment of human existence. It transforms our understanding of success and failure, redefines our concept of achievement, and provides an unwavering standard by which to evaluate our choices and actions. In a world often characterized by spiritual confusion and material excess, this promise stands as a beacon, guiding the believers toward their true home and ultimate destiny.

Discussion Questions

1. How might our daily lives transform if we truly internalized the reality that each action either brings us closer to or further from seeing Allah? Consider specific situations where this awareness might alter our choices.
2. In what ways does the promise of seeing Allah ﷻ transcend all other rewards of Paradise, and how does this understanding affect our perspective on worldly challenges and sacrifices?
3. Reflect on the honor of being among those whom Allah ﷻ will praise for worshipping Him without seeing Him. How does this recognition influence our approach to maintaining faith during times of difficulty or doubt?

"O Allah, I ask You for the joy of looking upon Your Face and the longing to meet You, without harmful adversity or misleading trials."

27

Trust in the Promise

In early 2020, just before the global lockdowns, an elderly man stood before the Kaʿbah, tears streaming down his weathered face. For sixty years, Omar had dreamed of this moment. Sixty years of saving coins in a jar marked "House of Allah." Sixty years of watching others return from Hajj while he remained behind.

Now, at eighty-three, having survived a heart attack that doctors said should have killed him, he finally stood here. His hands trembled as he raised them in du'aa, overwhelmed by the realization that every divine promise he had read in the Qur'an was as real as the sacred structure before him.

"Ya Allah," he whispered, his voice breaking, "You promised You would make a way for those who trust You. You promised patience would be rewarded. You promised You hear every du'aa. I stand here as proof that Your promises are true."

A young man beside him, moved by the elder's emotion, asked gently, "Uncle, what took you so long to get here?"

Omar smiled through his tears. "My son, I wasn't just traveling to Makkah. I was learning to trust. Every year that passed, every disappointment when I couldn't afford the journey, every time I put my family's needs before this dream taught me something. The journey here took sixty years, but the journey to trusting Allah's promises? That's what really brought me home."

He then recited, his voice carrying the weight of lived experience:

فَٱصْبِرْ إِنَّ وَعْدَ ٱللَّهِ حَقٌّ وَلَا يَسْتَخِفَّنَّكَ ٱلَّذِينَ لَا يُوقِنُونَ

"So be patient, for the promise of Allah certainly is true. And do not be disturbed by those who have no sure faith." (30:60)

These words from Surat al-Rūm represent the culmination of every promise we've explored in this book, every divine guarantee that has sustained believers through fourteen centuries. In a world that constantly whispers "maybe," Allah declares with absolute certainty: "My promise *is* true." Not probably true. Not conditionally true. Simply true.

This truth sustained Bilal under the scorching stones of Makkah. It gave Sumayyah the strength to become Islam's first martyr. It carries modern believers through cancer wards and refugee camps, through bankruptcy and betrayal, through every dark night that makes us wonder if dawn will ever come.

The context of this verse speaks directly to our times. Surat al-Rūm began with a promise that seemed impossible: that the defeated Romans would achieve victory within a few years. The pagans mocked this prediction. Yet when it came to pass exactly as foretold, it stood as eternal proof that when Allah promises something, the impossible becomes inevitable.

When Everything Seems Lost

Umm 'Azzam discovered the power of this promise through unbearable loss. When her husband and three sons were killed in a bombing, she felt her faith shatter. "I couldn't pray properly," she recalled. "I couldn't pray without feeling angry about my fate. Every promise I had believed felt like an illusion."

But in her darkest moment, curled on her prayer mat unable to form words, she remembered one promise: "Verily, with hardship comes ease." She couldn't feel it. But she whispered it anyway, over and over, like a drowning person clutching driftwood. "That tiny act of trust, even when I felt nothing, was like striking a match in absolute darkness," she explained. "The light was small, barely visible, but it was there. Each day I chose to trust just a little more, the light grew stronger. Now, five years later, I counsel other grieving mothers. I tell them: start with just one promise. Trust it even when you can't feel it. Watch how Allah responds to even that mustard seed of faith."

This is the divine formula hidden in trust: the more you rely on Allah's promises, the more light He places in your heart. And with more light comes greater capacity to persevere. It builds upon itself, carrying believers from strength to strength, from certainty to greater certainty. And with it, in holding, is eternal reward.

The Voices of Doubt

The verse warns us about those who "have no sure faith" trying to disturb our certainty. These aren't always aggressive critics in our lives, if we consider various manifestations for the sake of wider application. Sometimes they're the subtle voices of a materialistic society that measures everything by immediate, visible results. Sometimes they're our own internal whispers when prayers seem unanswered. Sometimes they're well-meaning friends who say "be realistic" when what they mean is "stop trusting in the unseen."

But notice Allah's instruction: He doesn't say these voices won't exist. He simply says don't let them disturb you. The Arabic word "*yastakhiffannaka*" implies being made light, unstable, easily moved. In other words, let the doubters doubt. You stand firm on the foundation of divine promise.

Today we face our own "impossible" moments. The young woman told she'll never conceive. The refugee dreaming of stability while living in his fourth temporary shelter. The convert whose family has disowned them, wondering if they'll ever belong again. To each of these souls, Allah says: "My promise is true."

This trust doesn't require the absence of doubt. Trust isn't about never wondering; it's about always returning to the truth despite our questions, with sincerity and humility.

The Promise Keeper

Throughout this book, we've explored Allah's magnificent promises. His promise to answer our prayers, though the answer might come in forms we don't expect. His promise to forgive all sins for those who sincerely repent. His promise to replace whatever we give in charity. His promise to grant ease after every hardship. His promise to reunite believing families in Paradise.

What makes these promises different from every human guarantee is that the One making them does not lie, does not forget, and cannot be prevented from fulfilling them. When Allah promises something, it doesn't depend on economic conditions, political stability, or any earthly variable. His promises transcend every limitation that makes human promises fragile.

The Creator of every atom in existence, the Sustainer of every beating heart, the Knower of every unspoken thought, has made personal promises to you. And He has never and will never break a single one.

This is why believers throughout history have accomplished the impossible. Not because they were superhuman, but because they were powered by trust in superhuman promises. The companions who memorized the entire Qur'an when books were luxury items. The scholars who traveled years on foot to verify single hadiths. The ordinary believers who chose torture over denying their faith. All were sustained by certainty that Allah's promises are true.

The Meeting

As you close this book and return to daily life, remember that every divine promise points to the ultimate promise: the meeting with Allah. After a lifetime of trusting what you couldn't see, you'll finally see the One you trusted. After years of believing in promises others called fantasy, you'll find yourself in the reality they all pointed toward. After every moment of choosing faith over doubt, patience over despair, trust over fear, you'll hear the words every believer longs for:

يَـٰٓأَيَّتُهَا ٱلنَّفْسُ ٱلْمُطْمَئِنَّةُ ٱرْجِعِىٓ إِلَىٰ رَبِّكِ رَاضِيَةً مَّرْضِيَّةً

فَٱدْخُلِى فِى عِبَـٰدِى وَٱدْخُلِى جَنَّتِى

"O tranquil soul! Return to your Lord, well pleased ˹with Him˺ and well pleasing ˹to Him˺. So join My servants, and enter My Paradise." (89:27-30)

This is not wishful thinking. This is the promise of the One who created you, sustained you, and has been guiding you home through every promise in this book. The journey might be long. The path might be difficult. But the destination is certain for those who trust.

So be patient. The promise of Allah is true. More true than the ground beneath your feet. More true than the challenges you're facing. Let every difficulty become an opportunity to declare: "I trust Allah's promise." Let every blessing become a moment to affirm: "Allah's promise is fulfilled."

This is your inheritance as a believer: not just Paradise, but the unshakeable certainty that Paradise is real and waiting. Not just divine help, but the absolute assurance that help is already on its way. Not just eventual justice, but the peace that comes from knowing justice is guaranteed.

The promise of Allah is true. And that truth changes everything.

Discussion Questions

1. What long-held dream or unanswered prayer in your life might be teaching you a deeper lesson about trust? How can you reframe waiting as spiritual growth rather than delay?
2. When have you had to choose trust despite overwhelming emotion telling you otherwise? What was the outcome?
3. How would your approach to current anxieties change if you truly internalized that Allah's promises transcend all human limitations? What specific worry would lose its power over you?

"O Allah, make us among those who trust Your promises completely, who find strength in Your guarantees, and who live with the certainty that Your word is always true."

Glossary

Ākhirah (الآخِرَة) - The Hereafter; the eternal life after death.

Barakat (بَرَكَات) - Blessings; divine favor that brings increase and goodness.

Bid' (بِضْع) - A few; specifically referring to a number between three and nine.

Dhikr (ذِكْر) - Remembrance of Allah; the practice of reciting prayers, Qur'anic verses, or divine names.

Du'ā' (دُعَاء) - Supplication; personal prayer made to Allah.

Fajr (فَجْر) - Dawn; the first of the five daily prayers performed before sunrise.

Furqān (فُرْقَان) - Criterion; divine discernment that distinguishes between truth and falsehood.

Ḥadīth (حَدِيث) - Authenticated sayings, actions, or approvals of Prophet Muhammad ﷺ.

Ḥadīth Qudsī (حَدِيث قُدْسِيّ) - Sacred hadith; divine revelation expressed in the Prophet's words.

Ḥajj (حَجّ) - The annual pilgrimage to Makkah, one of Islam's five pillars.

Ḥalāl (حَلَال) - Lawful; permissible according to Islamic law.

Ḥaqq (حَقّ) - Truth; reality; that which is absolute and certain.

Ḥasanāt (حَسَنَات) - Good deeds; virtuous actions that earn divine reward.

Iḥsān (إِحْسَان) - Excellence in worship; worshipping Allah ﷻ as if seeing Him.

Īmān (إِيمَان) - Faith; belief in Allah and His teachings.

In shā'Allah (إِن شَاءَ الله) - God willing; hope with submission to divine will.

Istighfār (اسْتِغْفَار) - Seeking forgiveness from Allah.

Istiqāmah (اسْتِقَامَة) - Steadfastness; consistency in following the straight path.

Jannah (جَنَّة) - Paradise; the eternal garden promised to the righteous.

Jihād (جِهَاد) - Struggle; effort in the path of Allah, both internal and external.

Khalīfah (خَلِيفَة) - Vicegerent; steward; humanity's role as trustees on earth.

Lā ilāha illā Allah (لَا إِلَٰهَ إِلَّا الله) - There is no deity except Allah; the fundamental declaration of Islamic monotheism.

Muḥsinīn (مُحْسِنِين) - Those who do good; righteous deeds with excellence.

Nūr (نُور) - Light; divine illumination and guidance.

Qadar (قَدَر) - Divine decree; Allah's predetermined plan for all creation.

Qanā'ah (قَنَاعَة) - Contentment; satisfaction with what Allah has provided.

Ribā (رِبَا) - Interest; usury; prohibited in Islamic finance.

Ṣabr (صَبْر) - Patience; steadfast perseverance through difficulties.

Ṣadaqah (صَدَقَة) - Charity; voluntary giving for Allah's sake.

Ṣalāh (صَلَاة) - Prayer; the second pillar of Islam, performed five times daily.

Sayyi'āt (سَيِّئَات) - Evil deeds; sinful actions that earn divine displeasure.

Shahādah (شَهَادَة) - Testimony of faith; declaration that there is no god but Allah and Muhammad is His messenger.

Sharī'ah (شَرِيعَة) - Islamic law; divine guidance for human conduct.

Shirk (شِرْك) - Associating partners with Allah; the greatest sin in Islam.

Shukr (شُكْر) - Gratitude; expressed through heart, tongue, and actions.

Sujūd (سُجُود) - Prostration; the prayer position with the forehead on the ground.

Sunnah (سُنَّة) - The way of Prophet Muhammad ﷺ; his teachings and example.

Tafsīr (تَفْسِير) - Qur'anic commentary; scholarly interpretation of the Qur'an.

Taqwā (تَقْوَى) - God-consciousness; mindfulness of Allah leading to righteous conduct.

Tawakkul (تَوَكُّل) - Trust in Allah; reliance while taking appropriate action.

Tawbah (تَوْبَة) - Repentance; turning back to Allah after sin.

Ummah (أُمَّة) - Community; the global community of Muslims.

Waʿd (وَعْد) - Promise; divine assurance given by Allah.

Wa'īd (وَعِيد) - Warning; divine threat of punishment for disobedience.

Zakāh (زَكَاة) - Obligatory charity; a pillar requiring annual giving to the poor.

Ẓulm (ظُلْم) - Oppression; injustice; wrongdoing against others or oneself.

Index of Qur'anic Verses

So remember Me; I will remember you. And be grateful to Me and do not deny Me. (2:152)

فَاذْكُرُونِي أَذْكُرْكُمْ وَاشْكُرُوا لِي وَلَا تَكْفُرُونِ

When My servants ask you about Me: I am truly near. I respond to one's prayer when they call upon Me. (2:186)

وَإِذَا سَأَلَكَ عِبَادِي عَنِّي فَإِنِّي قَرِيبٌ أُجِيبُ دَعْوَةَ الدَّاعِ إِذَا دَعَانِ

Allah is the Guardian of those who believe. He brings them out from darkness into light. (2:257)

اللَّهُ وَلِيُّ الَّذِينَ آمَنُوا يُخْرِجُهُم مِّنَ الظُّلُمَاتِ إِلَى النُّورِ

The example of those who spend their wealth in the way of Allah is like a seed that grows seven spikes; in each spike is a hundred grains. (2:261)

مَّثَلُ الَّذِينَ يُنفِقُونَ أَمْوَالَهُمْ فِي سَبِيلِ اللَّهِ كَمَثَلِ حَبَّةٍ أَنبَتَتْ سَبْعَ سَنَابِلَ فِي كُلِّ سُنبُلَةٍ مِّائَةُ حَبَّةٍ

If you disclose your charitable expenditures, they are good; but if you conceal them and give them to the poor, it is better for you. (2:271)

إِن تُبْدُوا الصَّدَقَاتِ فَنِعِمَّا هِيَ ۖ وَإِن تُخْفُوهَا وَتُؤْتُوهَا الْفُقَرَاءَ فَهُوَ خَيْرٌ لَّكُمْ

Never will you attain righteousness until you spend from that which you love. (3:92)

لَن تَنَالُوا الْبِرَّ حَتَّىٰ تُنفِقُوا مِمَّا تُحِبُّونَ

Those who spend during ease and hardship and who restrain anger and who pardon the people. (3:134)

الَّذِينَ يُنفِقُونَ فِي السَّرَّاءِ وَالضَّرَّاءِ وَالْكَاظِمِينَ الْغَيْظَ وَالْعَافِينَ عَنِ النَّاسِ

And whoever does wrong or wrongs himself but then seeks forgiveness of Allah will find Allah Forgiving and Merciful. (4:110)

وَمَن يَعْمَلْ سُوءًا أَوْ يَظْلِمْ نَفْسَهُ ثُمَّ يَسْتَغْفِرِ اللَّهَ يَجِدِ اللَّهَ غَفُورًا رَّحِيمًا

Allah has promised those who believe and do good His forgiveness and a great reward. (4:122)

وَعَدَ ٱللَّهُ ٱلَّذِينَ ءَامَنُوا۟ وَعَمِلُوا۟ ٱلصَّٰلِحَٰتِ لَهُم مَّغْفِرَةٌ وَأَجْرٌ عَظِيمٌ

O you who believe! If you fear Allah, He will grant you a furqān, remove your evil deeds from you, and forgive you. (8:29)

يَا أَيُّهَا الَّذِينَ آمَنُوا إِن تَتَّقُوا اللَّهَ يَجْعَل لَّكُمْ فُرْقَانًا وَيُكَفِّرْ عَنكُمْ سَيِّئَاتِكُمْ وَيَغْفِرْ لَكُمْ

Allah has promised the believers, both men and women, Gardens under which rivers flow, to stay there forever, and splendid homes in the Gardens of Eternity, and—above all—the pleasure of Allah. (9:72)

وَعَدَ ٱللَّهُ ٱلْمُؤْمِنِينَ وَٱلْمُؤْمِنَٰتِ جَنَّٰتٍ تَجْرِى مِن تَحْتِهَا ٱلْأَنْهَٰرُ خَٰلِدِينَ فِيهَا وَمَسَٰكِنَ طَيِّبَةً فِى جَنَّٰتِ عَدْنٍ ۚ وَرِضْوَٰنٌ مِّنَ ٱللَّهِ أَكْبَرُ

Those who do good will have the finest reward and even more. (10:26)

لِّلَّذِينَ أَحْسَنُوا۟ ٱلْحُسْنَىٰ وَزِيَادَةٌ

Indeed, Allah will not change the condition of a people until they change what is in themselves. (13:11)

إِنَّ اللَّهَ لَا يُغَيِّرُ مَا بِقَوْمٍ حَتَّىٰ يُغَيِّرُوا مَا بِأَنفُسِهِمْ

Truly, in the remembrance of Allah do hearts find rest. (13:28)

أَلَا بِذِكْرِ اللَّهِ تَطْمَئِنُّ الْقُلُوبُ

And remember when your Lord proclaimed, "If you are grateful, I will certainly give you more. But if you are ungrateful, surely My punishment is severe." (14:7)

وَإِذْ تَأَذَّنَ رَبُّكُمْ لَئِن شَكَرْتُمْ لَأَزِيدَنَّكُمْ وَلَئِن كَفَرْتُمْ إِنَّ عَذَابِي لَشَدِيدٌ

And if you should count the favors of Allah, you could not enumerate them. (14:34)

وَإِن تَعُدُّوا نِعْمَةَ اللَّهِ لَا تُحْصُوهَا

And never think that Allah is unaware of what the wrongdoers do. He only delays them for a Day when eyes will stare in horror. (14:42)

وَلَا تَحْسَبَنَّ ٱللَّهَ غَٰفِلًا عَمَّا يَعْمَلُ ٱلظَّٰلِمُونَ ۚ إِنَّمَا يُؤَخِّرُهُمْ لِيَوْمٍ تَشْخَصُ فِيهِ ٱلْأَبْصَٰرُ

Whoever does good, whether male or female, and is a believer, We will surely bless them with a good life. (16:97)

مَنْ عَمِلَ صَالِحًا مِّن ذَكَرٍ أَوْ أُنثَىٰ وَهُوَ مُؤْمِنٌ فَلَنُحْيِيَنَّهُۥ حَيَاةً طَيِّبَةً

Every soul will taste death. And We test you with good and evil as a trial, then to Us you will all be returned. (21:35)

كُلُّ نَفْسٍ ذَائِقَةُ الْمَوْتِ وَنَبْلُوكُم بِالشَّرِّ وَالْخَيْرِ فِتْنَةً وَإِلَيْنَا تُرْجَعُونَ

There is no deity except You; exalted are You. Indeed, I have been of the wrongdoers. (21:87)

لَّا إِلَٰهَ إِلَّا أَنتَ سُبْحَانَكَ إِنِّي كُنتُ مِنَ الظَّالِمِينَ

Let them pardon and forgive. Do you not love that Allah should forgive you? And Allah is Forgiving and Merciful. (24:22)

وَلْيَعْفُوا وَلْيَصْفَحُوا أَلَا تُحِبُّونَ أَن يَغْفِرَ اللَّهُ لَكُمْ وَاللَّهُ غَفُورٌ رَّحِيمٌ

Allah has promised those of you who believe and do good that He will certainly make them successors in the land. (24:55)

وَعَدَ اللَّهُ ٱلَّذِينَ ءَامَنُوا مِنكُمْ وَعَمِلُوا ٱلصَّٰلِحَٰتِ لَيَسْتَخْلِفَنَّهُمْ فِى ٱلْأَرْضِ

Except for those who repent, believe, and do righteous deeds. For them, Allah will replace their evil deeds with good deeds. (25:70)

إِلَّا مَن تَابَ وَآمَنَ وَعَمِلَ عَمَلًا صَالِحًا فَأُولَٰئِكَ يُبَدِّلُ اللَّهُ سَيِّئَاتِهِمْ حَسَنَاتٍ

Whoever comes with a good deed will be rewarded with what is better, and they will be secure from the horror on that Day. (27:89)

مَن جَآءَ بِٱلْحَسَنَةِ فَلَهُۥ خَيْرٌ مِّنْهَا وَهُم مِّن فَزَعٍ يَوْمَئِذٍ ءَامِنُونَ

Do people think that they will be left alone because they say: "We believe" and will not be tested? (29:2)

أَحَسِبَ النَّاسُ أَن يُتْرَكُوا أَن يَقُولُوا آمَنَّا وَهُمْ لَا يُفْتَنُونَ

As for those who struggle in Our cause, We will surely guide them along Our Way. And Allah is certainly with the good-doers. (29:69)

وَالَّذِينَ جَاهَدُوا فِينَا لَنَهْدِيَنَّهُمْ سُبُلَنَا وَإِنَّ اللَّهَ لَمَعَ الْمُحْسِنِينَ

Corruption has spread on land and sea as a result of what people's hands have done, so that Allah may cause them to taste some of their deeds and perhaps they might return. (30:41)

ظَهَرَ الْفَسَادُ فِي الْبَرِّ وَالْبَحْرِ بِمَا كَسَبَتْ أَيْدِي النَّاسِ لِيُذِيقَهُم بَعْضَ الَّذِي عَمِلُوا لَعَلَّهُمْ يَرْجِعُونَ

So be patient, for the promise of Allah certainly is true. And do not be disturbed by those who have no sure faith. (30:60)

فَٱصْبِرْ إِنَّ وَعْدَ ٱللَّهِ حَقٌّ وَلَا يَسْتَخِفَّنَّكَ ٱلَّذِينَ لَا يُوقِنُونَ

No soul knows what has been hidden for them of comfort for eyes as reward for what they used to do. (32:17)

فَلَا تَعْلَمُ نَفْسٌ مَّآ أُخْفِيَ لَهُم مِّن قُرَّةِ أَعْيُنٍ جَزَآءًۢ بِمَا كَانُوا۟ يَعْمَلُونَ

Say, "Surely it is my Lord Who gives abundant or limited provisions to whoever He wills of His servants. And whatever you spend in charity, He will compensate you for it. For He is the Best Provider." (34:39)

قُلْ إِنَّ رَبِّي يَبْسُطُ الرِّزْقَ لِمَن يَشَاءُ مِنْ عِبَادِهِ وَيَقْدِرُ لَهُ وَمَا أَنفَقْتُم مِّن شَيْءٍ فَهُوَ يُخْلِفُهُ وَهُوَ خَيْرُ الرَّازِقِينَ

O humanity! Indeed, Allah's promise is true. So do not let the life of this world deceive you, nor let the Chief Deceiver deceive you about Allah. (35:5)

يَٰٓأَيُّهَا ٱلنَّاسُ إِنَّ وَعْدَ ٱللَّهِ حَقٌّ فَلَا تَغُرَّنَّكُمُ ٱلْحَيَوٰةُ ٱلدُّنْيَا وَلَا يَغُرَّنَّكُم بِٱللَّهِ ٱلْغَرُورُ

Say, "O My servants who have transgressed against themselves, do not despair of the mercy of Allah. Indeed, Allah forgives all sins." (39:53)

قُلْ يَا عِبَادِيَ الَّذِينَ أَسْرَفُوا عَلَىٰ أَنفُسِهِمْ لَا تَقْنَطُوا مِن رَّحْمَةِ اللَّهِ ۚ إِنَّ اللَّهَ يَغْفِرُ الذُّنُوبَ جَمِيعًا

Your Lord has proclaimed, "Call upon Me, I will respond to you. Surely those who are too proud to worship Me will enter Hell, fully humbled." (40:60)

وَقَالَ رَبُّكُمُ ادْعُونِي أَسْتَجِبْ لَكُمْ ۚ إِنَّ الَّذِينَ يَسْتَكْبِرُونَ عَنْ عِبَادَتِي سَيَدْخُلُونَ جَهَنَّمَ دَاخِرِينَ

Surely those who say, "Our Lord is Allah," and then remain steadfast, the angels descend upon them, saying, "Do not fear, nor grieve. Rather, rejoice in the good news of Paradise." (41:30)

إِنَّ الَّذِينَ قَالُوا رَبُّنَا اللَّهُ ثُمَّ اسْتَقَامُوا تَتَنَزَّلُ عَلَيْهِمُ الْمَلَائِكَةُ أَلَّا تَخَافُوا وَلَا تَحْزَنُوا وَأَبْشِرُوا بِالْجَنَّةِ الَّتِي كُنتُمْ تُوعَدُونَ

Whatever affliction befalls you is because of what your own hands have committed. And He pardons much. (42:30)

وَمَا أَصَابَكُم مِّن مُّصِيبَةٍ فَبِمَا كَسَبَتْ أَيْدِيكُمْ وَيَعْفُو عَن كَثِيرٍ

Believers, if you aid Allah, He will come to your aid and will plant your feet firmly. (47:7)

يَا أَيُّهَا الَّذِينَ آمَنُوا إِن تَنصُرُوا اللَّهَ يَنصُرْكُمْ وَيُثَبِّتْ أَقْدَامَكُمْ

As for those who are rightly guided, He increases them in guidance and blesses them with righteousness. (47:17)

وَالَّذِينَ اهْتَدَوْا زَادَهُمْ هُدًى وَآتَاهُمْ تَقْوَاهُمْ

Indeed, Allah will fulfill His Messenger's vision in all truth: Allah willing, you will surely enter the Sacred Mosque, in security. (48:27)

لَّقَدْ صَدَقَ ٱللَّهُ رَسُولَهُ ٱلرُّءْيَا بِٱلْحَقِّ لَتَدْخُلُنَّ ٱلْمَسْجِدَ ٱلْحَرَامَ إِن شَآءَ ٱللَّهُ ءَامِنِينَ

As for those who believe and whose descendants follow them in faith, We will elevate their descendants to their rank. (52:21)

وَٱلَّذِينَ ءَامَنُوا۟ وَٱتَّبَعَتْهُمْ ذُرِّيَّتُهُم بِإِيمَـٰنٍ أَلْحَقْنَا بِهِمْ ذُرِّيَّتَهُمْ

Every being on earth is bound to perish. Only your Lord Himself, full of Majesty and Honor, will remain forever. (55:26-27)

كُلُّ مَنْ عَلَيْهَا فَانٍ وَيَبْقَىٰ وَجْهُ رَبِّكَ ذُو الْجَلَالِ وَالْإِكْرَامِ

And whoever is mindful of Allah, He will make a way out for them, and provide for them from sources they could never imagine. (65:2-3)

وَمَن يَتَّقِ ٱللَّهَ يَجْعَل لَّهُۥ مَخْرَجًا وَيَرْزُقْهُ مِنْ حَيْثُ لَا يَحْتَسِبُ

On that Day some faces will be radiant and bright, looking at their Lord. (75:22-23)

وُجُوهٌ يَوْمَئِذٍ نَّاضِرَةٌ إِلَىٰ رَبِّهَا نَاظِرَةٌ

We fear from our Lord a terribly distressful Day; so Allah will deliver them from the horror of that Day, and grant them radiance and joy. (76:10-11)

إِنَّا نَخَافُ مِن رَّبِّنَا يَوْمًا عَبُوسًا قَمْطَرِيرًا فَوَقَىٰهُمُ ٱللَّهُ شَرَّ ذَٰلِكَ ٱلْيَوْمِ وَلَقَّىٰهُمْ نَضْرَةً وَسُرُورًا

Indeed, with hardship comes ease. (94:5)

إِنَّ مَعَ الْعُسْرِ يُسْرًا

ABOUT THE AUTHOR

Dr. Suleiman Hani is an international lecturer, scholar-in-residence, the Dean of Academic Affairs at AlMaghrib Institute, and a leadership consultant and board adviser to numerous organizations. At the age of fourteen, he completed a Qur'an memorization program and went on to study under numerous scholars, earning dozens of traditional certifications in the Islamic sciences. He later obtained a master's degree from the University of Jordan's College of Sharīʿah, a second master's degree from Harvard University, and a doctorate in leadership from New York University. Over the past decade, he has served as a resident scholar in Michigan, lectured in dozens of countries worldwide, published several works, and appeared on major Islamic TV networks.

In addition to this book, Shaykh Suleiman is the author of other bestselling titles:

1. 114 Tips to Help You *Finally* Memorize the Qur'an
2. The Iron Healing: Lessons & Reflections from Surah al-Hadid
   With 120 Discussion Questions & Mastery Tracker
3. Special Virtues of the Qur'an's Chapters & Verses
   Foreword by Dr. Omar Suleiman
4. The Golden Chain Narrations
   81 Prophetic Wisdoms through Abdullah b. Umar (ra)
5. Fiqh al-Muwazanat: The Jurisprudence of Weighing Benefits & Harms
   Foreword by Dr. Hatem Al-Haj

For more information, visit **imamsuleiman.com**

Endnotes

[1] Walter Kaegi, *Byzantium and the Early Islamic Conquests* (1992), 32.
[2] Sebeos, *The Armenian History Attributed to Sebeos* (1999).
[3] Sebeos, *Armenian History,* 212.
[4] Sebeos, *Armenian History*, 187.
[5] Parvaneh Pourshariati, *Decline and Fall of the Sasanian Empire* (2008).
[6] Jāmiʿ al-Tirmidhī.
[7] Jāmiʿ al-Tirmidhī.
[8] Abu Ja'far al-Tabari, *Jami' al-bayan,* 30:1-5.
[9] Sebeos, *Armenian History*, xxiv.
[10] Pourshariati, *Decline,* 1-2.
[11] Jāmiʿ al-Tirmidhī.
[12] Ṣaḥīḥ al-Bukhārī.
[13] Ṣaḥīḥ al-Bukhārī.
[14] Ṣaḥīḥ al-Bukhārī.
[15] Ṣaḥīḥ Muslim.
[16] Ṣaḥīḥ al-Bukhārī.
[17] Ṣaḥīḥ Muslim.
[18] Ṣaḥīḥ al-Bukhārī.
[19] Ṣaḥīḥ Muslim.
[20] Jāmiʿ al-Tirmidhī.
[21] Ṣaḥīḥ al-Bukhārī.
[22] Jāmiʿ al-Tirmidhī.
[23] Ṣaḥīḥ Muslim.
[24] Ibn al-Qayyim, *Madarij al-Sālikīn.*
[25] al-Bayhaqī, *Al-Zuhd.*
[26] Ṣaḥīḥ Muslim.
[27] Attributed to Umar (ra), but the chain of narration is cut off and thus it is considered weak. Its meaning is undoubtedly true. See Ibn al-Mubārak, *Al-Zuhd.*
[28] Jāmiʿ al-Tirmidhī.
[29] Jāmiʿ al-Tirmidhī.
[30] Musnad Aḥmad.
[31] Jāmiʿ al-Tirmidhī.
[32] Jāmiʿ al-Tirmidhī.
[33] Jāmiʿ al-Tirmidhī.
[34] Ṣaḥīḥ al-Bukhārī.
[35] Abū Nuʿaym, *Ḥilyat al-Awliyāʾ.*
[36] Jāmiʿ al-Tirmidhī.
[37] Jāmiʿ al-Tirmidhī.
[38] Ṣaḥīḥ al-Bukhārī.
[39] Jāmiʿ al-Tirmidhī.
[40] Ṣaḥīḥ Muslim.
[41] Jāmiʿ al-Tirmidhī.
[42] al-Ṭabarānī.
[43] Ṣaḥīḥ Muslim.
[44] Ṣaḥīḥ Muslim.
[45] Ṣaḥīḥ Muslim.
[46] Jāmiʿ al-Tirmidhī.
[47] Ṣaḥīḥ al-Bukhārī.
[48] Ṣaḥīḥ Muslim.
[49] Sunan al-Nasā'ī.
[50] Ṣaḥīḥ al-Bukhārī.
[51] Ṣaḥīḥ al-Bukhārī.
[52] Ṣaḥīḥ Muslim.
[53] Ṣaḥīḥ Muslim.
[54] al-Ṭabarānī.
[55] Ṣaḥīḥ al-Bukhārī.
[56] Ṣaḥīḥ al-Bukhārī.
[57] Ibn al-Qayyim, *al-Wābil al-Ṣaʾib.*
[58] Ṣaḥīḥ Muslim.
[59] Ṣaḥīḥ al-Bukhārī.
[60] Ṣaḥīḥ al-Bukhārī.
[61] Ṣaḥīḥ al-Bukhārī.
[62] Sunan Ibn Mājah.
[63] Ṣaḥīḥ al-Bukhārī.
[64] Ṣaḥīḥ Muslim.
[65] Ṣaḥīḥ Muslim.
[66] Ṣaḥīḥ Muslim.
[67] Jāmiʿ al-Tirmidhī.
[68] Ṣaḥīḥ al-Bukhārī.
[69] Ṣaḥīḥ al-Bukhārī.
[70] Jāmiʿ al-Tirmidhī.
[71] Ṣaḥīḥ al-Bukhārī.
[72] Jāmiʿ al-Tirmidhī.
[73] Ṣaḥīḥ al-Bukhārī.
[74] Ṣaḥīḥ al-Bukhārī.
[75] Ṣaḥīḥ Muslim.
[76] Ṣaḥīḥ Muslim.
[77] Jāmiʿ al-Tirmidhī.
[78] Jāmiʿ al-Tirmidhī.
[79] Ṣaḥīḥ al-Bukhārī.
[80] Ṣaḥīḥ Muslim.
[81] Jāmiʿ al-Tirmidhī.
[82] Ṣaḥīḥ al-Bukhārī.
[83] Sunan Ibn Mājah.
[84] Jāmiʿ al-Tirmidhī.
[85] Sunan Ibn Mājah.
[86] Jāmiʿ al-Tirmidhī.
[87] Ṣaḥīḥ al-Bukhārī.
[88] Ṣaḥīḥ al-Bukhārī.
[89] Ṣaḥīḥ Muslim.
[90] al-Ṭabarī, *Jāmiʿ al-Bayān*, on Q 41:30.
[91] al-Ṭabarī, ibid.
[92] al-Ṭabarī, ibid.
[93] Ibn Rajab, *Majmūʿ Rasāʾil.*
[94] al-Ṭabarī, *Jāmiʿ al-Bayān,* on Q 41:30.
[95] Ṣaḥīḥ al-Bukhārī.
[96] al-Dhahabī, *Siyar Aʿlām al-Nubalāʾ.*
[97] Ṣaḥīḥ Muslim.
[98] Sunan al-Nasā'ī
[99] Ṣaḥīḥ al-Bukhārī.
[100] Ṣaḥīḥ al-Bukhārī.
[101] Ṣaḥīḥ al-Bukhārī.
[102] Ṣaḥīḥ al-Bukhārī.
[103] Ṣaḥīḥ al-Bukhārī.
[104] Ṣaḥīḥ al-Bukhārī.
[105] Ṣaḥīḥ Muslim.
[106] Jāmiʿ al-Tirmidhī.

www.ingramcontent.com/pod-product-compliance
Lightning Source LLC
Chambersburg PA
CBHW022114040426
42450CB00006B/693
* 9 7 8 1 9 6 9 3 5 8 0 0 5 *